Legacy:
60 Life Reflections for
the Next Generation

Other books by Stephen A. Macchia:

Becoming A Healthy Church

Becoming A Healthy Church Workbook

Becoming A Healthy Disciple

Becoming A Healthy Disciple: Small Group Study and Worship Guide

Becoming A Healthy Team

Becoming A Healthy Team Exercises

Crafting A Rule of Life

Wellspring: 31 Days to Whole Hearted Living

Path of a Beloved Disciple: 31 Days in the Gospel of John

Broken and Whole: A Leader's Path to Spiritual Transformation

Outstretched Arms of Grace: A 40-Day Lenten Devotional

Legacy:
60 Life Reflections for the Next Generation

Written On the Occasion of My 60th Birthday

by **Stephen A. Macchia,**
Grateful Father of Nathan and Rebekah

© 2017 by **Stephen A. Macchia**

Published by **Leadership Transformations (LTI Publications)**
P.O. Box 338, Lexington, MA 02420
www.leadershiptransformations.org

July 2017

Printed in the United States of America.

Library of Congress Cataloging-in-Publication Data
Macchia, Stephen A., 1956–
Legacy / Stephen A. Macchia.
Includes bibliographical references.

ISBN 978-0-692-91532-5 (pbk.)

Dedicated to my beloved parents and grandparents

With profound gratitude for their humble devotion to their family and friends, their commitment to their Christian faith and local church, and their unconditional and hospitable service to others

Their legacy lives on in our generation…with love, joy and thankfulness

Table of Contents

Introduction

I distinctly remember the day I turned 57…it was a jarring reality that I was indeed getting old. Before I knew it, I'd be 60 – yikes! Sure enough: all of a sudden I'm there! Recently, when I was chatting with my neighbors about my upcoming birthday – the big 6-0, they asked me what we'd be doing to celebrate. Their Korean cultural assumption: hosting a huge birthday party to commemorate coming "full circle" (as in the full 60 minutes of a clock hand), considered a great accomplishment and a high water mark. My immediate reaction: If 60 is at the top of the circle, will it all be downhill from there?

When my wife Ruth asked me if I wanted a party, I was clearly not inclined to be the center of attention for this birthday. When I was sharing with a good friend about turning 60, he thoughtfully asked me, "Well then, if not a party, then what do YOU want to do to celebrate turning 60?" It took me by surprise, but I subsequently gave myself permission to consider the question. As a result, there were indeed a few goals I wanted to achieve: one was professional, another included travel, a third was about our home, another was personal, and the rest were about my family.

One of my specific goals was to write the following reflections for my dearly loved children, Nathan and Rebekah. When I sat down to brainstorm what the categories and the sub-topics would be, I must admit: it flowed from somewhere deep within. All 12 categories and each of the 60 topics were decided in one setting. So, I knew that not only did I want to write these for my kids, I actually felt called to do so. Why else would God make it so crystal clear except that he was inviting me into this exercise and his Spirit would empower me to complete the task for his honor and glory?

And so I set out to write these short reflections to my children…and they are shared with a wider audience only as a source of encouragement, not necessarily to have these be the messages you would offer to your children, but to urge you to share what matters most to you with your offspring. Don't assume they know what's going on inside of you as you age: your legacy will be carried on no matter what. Why not help that legacy be remembered in ways you would prefer? So I'd like to invite you to consider the following musings as a source of inspiration to you at whatever inflection point or season of life you find yourself in the midst of today.

Let your life speak! The stories you impart today will last for many other lifetimes!

For Christ's Glory and my children's edification, and with timeless affection and love,

Stephen A. Macchia
Lexington, MA
August 22, 2016

How to Use This Book

What you're about to read are 60 pieces of wisdom and advice for my own children. Your own life experience has likely had its own twists and turns —some in common with mine and some very different. My hope is that what I've written to my own (adult) kids will stimulate your thinking and give you an opportunity to reflect upon and craft your own pieces of wisdom and advice that are important for you to pass on to your own children and grand-children. At the beginning of each section there is a "question to ponder" to help you think about these ideas as you read. At the end of each section there is a space called "What I'd like to add." In this space, I offer some questions to guide you in thinking about what and how to share your own legacy with your own offspring. Be as personal as you can in affirming and guiding your children and grandchildren in the advice that you give. Please use this as a starting point for your own ideas. I, as a pastor, ministry leader, and fledgling author, chose to communicate to my children through the written word. Some of you may not be writers, so as you read, think of what medium is best to communicate your own legacy. Perhaps you might want to use photographs, poetry, recorded messages, or other creative mediums to help guide you in this pilgrimage. Enjoy the process however God may lead you!

The original version of this book included a letter to each of my children which conveyed my delight in them as their father and my desire to pass along some important truths that could help them flourish in life and maybe even avoid a few potholes along the way. That letter has been removed in order to make space for you to write your own.

There is space on the next page for you to write your own brief intro-duction to your children/grandchildren. How do you wish to express to them your own feelings of love and delight in them as their parent/grandparent? How would you communicate to them your desire to share nuggets of wisdom with them that you hope they will cherish and benefit from for the rest of their lives? Perhaps you have a prayer to offer, a quip to share, or a quote to begin with…ask the Lord to guide you and lean in to what emerges.

A Letter to You,
My Beloved ...

_____

_____

_____

_____

_____

_____

_____

_____

_____

_____

_____

_____

_____

A Letter to You, My Beloved

Section I: Lessons Learned

"Trust in the Lord with all our heart and lean not on your own understanding; in all your ways submit to him, and he will make your paths straight."

— Proverbs 3: 5,6

Something to ponder as you read this section:

Which of your own life lessons would you like to impart to the next generation in your family?

1
Save for a rainy day

M y father (your Papa), Italo Macchia, grew up in the Depression. His father left the family he brought over to the USA from Italy shortly after getting them settled in the Italian quarter of Princeton, NJ. Papa did what he could - with the help of his siblings - to provide much needed financial resources for his beloved mother. They each worked extra jobs while going to school, and tirelessly served their mother and family. That's why Papa was always frugal about each dollar he earned, saved and spent. One of his famous sayings to your Aunties Janice, Carol and me was, "If you walk by a penny on the ground then it means you don't really care about the dollar in your pocket." I recall this each time I see a penny on the ground and when I pick it up I do so in your Papa's memory. His pennywise economics lesson has impacted my life significantly.

You didn't hear me say Papa's phrase to you very often as you grew up in our household, most likely because we did what we could to provide for all of your means. Your mom and I valued each dollar we earned, saved and spent. One habit we got into from the first week of our marriage was to account for each penny we spent. For many years we recorded these daily in a spiral bound notebook, and today we do so electronically. We tried our best not to complain about what we didn't have, but instead would focus on the blessings we received each season of our family's growth. As the years have progressed, many of our peers have acquired so much more than we have, but we count ourselves fortunate to be where we are today as a ministry family.

Knowing where your money comes from and where it eventually ends up, provides much needed information for what you can afford to purchase and invest along the way. So, my simple advice is this: account for your pennies (and your dollars); keep a simple budget for this season and the next; save as much as you can (remember the rule of compounding interest); live within your margins and avoid debt as much as possible (exceptions being a home and an automobile); and give to your church, favorite charitable organizations, and others in need as generously and hospitably as possible (we've taught you to tithe+ in hopes of you following this same objective with your loved ones). Caring about the dollars you are stewarding (working hard to earn, and then spending wisely and thoughtfully) today will come in handy when that inevitable rainy day occurs!

2

Be kind to all

One of my lifetime heroes was my beloved mother (your Nonna), Ruth Naomi Humbert Macchia. She enjoyed a simple, humble, gentle, generous, hospitable, and loving life, with deep roots in her Pennsylvania Dutch/ German Lutheran home. Her dad, my Grandpa, Oscar Jacob Humbert, was also one of my heroes. Both were so much alike, as my mom emulated her father, who worked for over 50 years for the Baltimore Sun Newspaper as a humble typesetter. She grew up in their home at 5510 Craig Avenue, just a few walkable blocks from their home church, Holy Comforter Lutheran Church, in downtown Baltimore. The family house sat gently on the corner of the avenue, with a grand front porch, lush gardens tended to by Grandpa, and delightful smells that came from the kitchen and welcomed us with grace-filled hospitality. Hers was a simple life, uncluttered by the things of this world, and yet rich in family love.

One of my mom's favorite sayings was on the subject of character, "You become like the people you hang around with and by what you fill your mind with." She never needed to preach this to us as children, but provided her typically gentle reminders whenever she heard about the kids we were befriending, the books we were (mostly not) reading, and the television shows we were watching. She had many friends herself, and when she passed away at the ripe age of 80, we knew she didn't leave behind a single enemy. Very simply, she was a delight to know and be with, no matter the condition of the "world" we were occupying at the time. My mom was always there to comfort us with loving words of affection and arms of loving embrace. Her lifestyle was always one of grace, kindness, compassion, and unconditional love.

She would never say "mean people stink," but that's my crass way of interpreting and stating the obvious. Our family has had our share of interaction with mean people, who in their rudeness are telling the world around them that they are miserable themselves (remember: hurting people hurt people). So, please avoid all ways of being mean yourself and stay far away from the attitudes of the mean people of this world (there are far too many!). And, recall what your mom and I have said to you many times over the years: Impact the world with kindness to all who cross your path and you'll be much happier as a result. Show kindness to all, even the stranger who is in need of a simple act of mercy. Expressing kind words, gestures, and deeds will go a long way in this unkind world in which we all inhabit. And, remember to hang out with those who bring out your best and help you laugh at yourself (not at others) with unspeakable joy. Live fully, laugh heartily, and choose daily to love kindly and abundantly!

3

Consider your life

One of the most significant secular business books I read as a young leader was written by a prolific Mormon business leader, Stephen Covey, entitled *Seven Habits of Highly Effective People*. In fact, I first read this book while on an airplane heading to what I thought was my proper destination for a speaking engagement the following morning: St. John, New Brunswick, Canada. Instead, I found myself landing in St. John's, Newfoundland, Canada...about 500 miles and a province away from where I was supposed to be. I was clueless I was heading in the wrong direction, unaware of my sense of direction (or lack thereof), or the amount of time it was taking me to reach my destination. I simply was along for the ride, oblivious to my environment, merely showing up to do what I thought I was supposed to do that particular Friday night.

It took me a while to discover my true geographical location, carrying around the airport baggage claim area my overnight bag and a box of literature for the seminar I was asked to teach the following morning. I wasn't inclined to ask for help in that foreign airport (mostly due to my male stubbornness), but eventually acquiesced to my conscience and sought the advice of an Air Canada official. She informed me of my dilemma: "No sir, you're in Newfoundland, not New Brunswick." Not knowing my Canadian geography, it took a while to realize my conundrum. To make a long story short, I flew for several hours on two wrong airplanes and ended up in a wrong destination...much to my chagrin. It was humiliating and frustrating and I felt like a fool.

The irony of my journey was the title of the book I was reading at the time, as I certainly didn't feel at all like an effective person. Since then, I have sought diligently to "begin with the end in mind" (one of Covey's truisms) so to avoid ending up in the wrong place at the wrong time. And I suggest you do the same. In all aspects of life: your personal life, immediate and extended family, your circle of friendships, your workplace, your church, your community, and even your participation in the wider world in which you contribute. I hope you will regularly assess and (re)consider your life...what kind of person do you want to become when all is said and done? Generous? Gracious? Godly? Gifted? And, what kind of life do you want to live? Abundant? Effective? Fruitful? Christlike? If so, then begin today to practice being that kind of person in your personal space and among all who you know, love and serve. Ending up in the right destination in life is always the best choice to make, but it takes some consideration of the direction you are heading in the first place.

4
Listen well

As you've undoubtedly heard me describe the ministry of Leadership Transformations and the various services we provide, the central message of our daily work focuses on one word: listen. I firmly believe that the most important leadership attribute is the ability to listen well. And, since we affirm together, "As the leader goes, so goes the organization...and, more importantly, as the soul of the leader goes, so goes the leader," I believe the soul is the most important part of the person (and often the most neglected). The soul that listens, first and foremost to God, is one that lovingly responds to what is heard (in prayer and in the Word), and then leads others to do likewise. It's out of our listening attentively to God first and foremost that we will learn how to live intentionally and love abundantly with the One who knows us first and pursues us continuously with the greatest of all intimacy and affection. This is the essence of holy listening, a practice I've sought to learn and to help others acquire. It's a life-changer.

The same goes for our human relationships. The one who listens well, leads and serves others out of a soulful life that's nurtured by what is received. When we listen attentively to one another, we discover the deepest longings of those we know, love and serve. But, listening well isn't something intuitively fulfilled, it takes practice. We need to learn how to listen to our family and friends; it doesn't come via osmosis or even in our upbringing (as important as our family of origin is in this regard). In fact, it's quite unlike the rest of our world, which focuses more on self rather than on others. However, what I've discovered over the years is that few of us want to be fixed, but all of us want to be listened to - yes, all of us. Therefore, listening is the best gift we can give another, whether that gift is offered to God, another person, or even yourself.

But, to really listen well we need to be present and focused, not absent and distracted. And that feels next to impossible in this world so filled with distractions, noise, and constant motion. It's rare to find a moment to ourselves, uninterrupted by technology or the needs of others clamoring for our attention. Our ability to be present-focused is curtailed by the constant barrage of stimuli in our world. But it's also challenged by our guilt and/or regret about the past, or our worry and/or concern about the future. To learn how to listen well means that we need to make radical, countercultural decisions to focus on this godly intention. Reflect often on the following very basic question: "Right now, am I fully present?" Only then can you practice the loving art of completely focused listening. Dear ones, let me encourage you to show your love for others by listening well. And I pray you'll have others in your life who will do the same for you. Remember too that you'll always have a listening ear to come home to – yes, always.

5

Guard your heart

One of the small devotionals I wrote is entitled *Wellspring* and it comes from the lovely proverb about guarding our heart, which is the wellspring of our lives (Proverbs 4:23). As our soul exclusively belongs to God, the Lover of our soul, our hearts are inclined toward both God and others...having both a vertical (upward toward God) and horizontal (sideways toward others) impact. At times our hearts are wicked, other times loving, but most of the time somewhere in between. Having a growing self-awareness is key...where is my heart right now? Inclined toward God and others in a loving manner, or dislocated and off the mark, distanced from God's heart and disenfranchised from what's best? When you purpose to guard your heart, you will remain mindful of where it's most inclined and deliberately choose to bring it back "home" into the embrace of God.

The truth of the matter is that our hearts need continuous reformation from the discombobulating influences of our day. We need to notice what's happening deep within our heart and soul and reconfigure or realign our heart's inclination according to what we know to be right, true, loving, and gracious. St. Augustine – who lived, wrote, and served in the early 400's AD – knew the condition of his heart and wrote about the need to reorder one's affections each new day, and even several times throughout the day. It's simply too easy to let our hearts lean in directions that are unhealthy for us, whether it be toward lesser loves or predispositions that lead to our destruction. And, given the reality of each person's heart, there is no one exempt from such temptation. That's what we all share in common as human beings in desperate need for God's heart to penetrate and transform our hearts daily.

The best way I know of guarding our hearts is through the care of our soul, by creating space for God – the Lover of your soul – to return once again to the center of our hearts. We can only do so in unhurried, uncluttered, unhindered spaciousness: a commodity not created or celebrated in our world today. We all need a sacred space, a set apart place where we can be alone with God and recline toward his Word, listen to his voice in prayer, and reflect upon the genuine condition of our heart. For many years that sacred space for me has been in our back room, at the end of the couch, facing out toward our backyard, where I can set apart time and space in my hectic life to simply be alone with God. There have been many days when I've been desperate for such a reprieve from the demands of others pulling on my soul. My prayer is that you too will indeed make this counter-cultural choice as regularly as possible. It won't be easy, as the demands to do otherwise will often outweigh this important priority. But, always remember: guard your heart, or all sorts of competing demons and demands of your day will inevitably eat it alive. Your heart is the true wellspring of your life. Guard it well, my children.

What I'd Like to add related to *Lessons Learned:*

Key lessons learned that my parents, grandparents, etc. passed down to me:

_____

_____

_____

_____

_____

_____

My own "school of hard knocks" lessons from which I would like to spare you:

_____

_____

_____

_____

_____

_____

_____

Values or lessons that we've held dearly in our family:

_____

_____

_____

_____

_____

_____

_____

_____

One piece of advice as you learn your own lessons:

_____

_____

_____

_____

_____

_____

_____

_____

Additional thoughts:

Section II:
Decisions Made

"Start children off on the way they should go, and even when they are old they will not turn from it."

— Proverbs 22:6

Something to ponder as you read this section: Which of your own major decisions would you like to recount with the next generation in your family?

6
Receive Jesus

When your "Uncle" Rich (Plass) first entered my life, I was a high school junior. A mere 16 years of age, but wide open and pliable to the gospel he presented and the discipleship he offered. I was hungry for what he provided to me in Christ, and I gratefully received the message of salvation from this impressive messenger of grace. I knew something was unique about this man of God, and what he presented was indeed complementary to my upbringing, but became even more transformative as our time together increased. I was raised in my loving family and as an active participant in the life of First Congregational Church in Stoneham, Massachusetts I was taught faithfully to know about, love, worship, and serve God. So when Uncle Rich suggested I could actually have a living relationship with the God I had been taught about, the decision to invite Jesus to reign supreme in my heart was both gracious and life-altering.

Receiving the loving message of Jesus from someone as receivable as Uncle Rich was seamless and just so right. The timing was ideal, the invitation was clear, and my heart was wide open and ready. I can still picture in my mind's eye the setting of the high school "Pilgrim Fellowship" room at the church, kneeling beside the beat up couch, after participating in a study in the gospel of John, and praying for Jesus to enter, occupy and transform my heart. Time stood still for that sacred moment. I knew my life would never be the same again. And that's truer than I could ever fully express. Receiving the love of Jesus released from deep within my soul a love for God that was incredibly significant and undoubtedly transformational. I have never even thought to reconsider that life-changing decision, even when heartache and disappointment come my way.

Your mother and I prayed for you before you were born, that you too would grow up to receive the love of Jesus, allow him to renew and transform you from the inside out, and walk with him for the rest of your life. Our hope all along was that you would trust Jesus to be the guardian of your heart and life as a result of what you heard and observed and received in our home. Your beautiful conversion stories of praying simple and faith-filled prayers led you to your baptism and into your life with God. My daily prayer is that you will deliberately, determinedly, and daily choose to receive all that Jesus chooses to give to you - the good, the hard, the meaningful, and the daily gifts he alone can provide. And, that in receiving from Jesus his life-changing presence, power and peace, you too will become receivable to others. Nothing is more important.

7

Marry up

As you well know, I married up. Your mother is one of the most amazing women to walk planet earth. When I first met her she and I were at Northwestern College in Orange City, Iowa. Uncle Rich had attended that school and he advised me to do likewise. I followed in his footsteps and it was one of the best decisions of my life. And, it was capped off in my senior year when I met your mom, Ruth Lynn. She and her girlfriends were at the local pizza ranch celebrating her birthday, when my buddy Larryl and I were invited to join their party. We started dating the following weekend at our Winter Carnival dance (mom would want me to tell you it was after that dance that I first kissed her, something she was shocked to receive so early on in our relationship!). Six months later we were engaged; a year later we were married. She's been my faithful lover, life partner and a consistent blessing to so many others and me for nearly four decades. I can attest to her inner strength and outer beauty as I've observed her daily life with joy.

Also as you well know, your mom had a hard life. The details of which are not mine to tell in written form. But, you know enough to make your head spin and your heart ache. She is a survivor who thrived against all the odds. She was watched over by a loving God and a handful of devoted Christ-followers who came to her aid at just the right times in her life, and for each of them we are eternally grateful. As a result of her beautiful perseverance, she is compassionate, gracious, loving, and available to others in need. She loves being surrounded by young moms and young children, and is especially encouraging to those who are doing their best to raise the next generation in ways that defy all the odds descending on them by every angle of our secular world. In a word: she gets it, having experienced so much pain and disappointment herself, and as a result many trust her with their story. God the Redeemer is at work in her life big time!

Our marriage has been rich and wonderful, but not at all absent of difficulty and challenge. We've encountered and endured our share of pain, heartache and disappointment. When others around us were blessed beyond measure, our biggest blessings seemed to come out of deep wounds that God alone could redeem and heal. None of these were considered from the beginning or created single handedly by us; all came toward us surprisingly: physical issues that Nate endured; psychological pathologies inflicted upon us by others; disappointments and even betrayals that emerged in unforeseen fashion. But, what has impressed me over and over again is how your mom both endured and survived them, with tested patience and God-given grace. If there's one important place to make sure you decide best, it's in the choice of a spouse. Nate, you have done so with Ashley and we love having her in our family and in your life (and I loved performing your marriage ceremony, thank you for one of the highlights of my life!). Bekah, don't ever forget that marrying up will keep you from falling down...love, joy, peace, commitment, courage, perseverance, and determination are keys to marital bliss. Pass this important message along to your children too, ok?

8

Love and serve the Church

Your dad is an EpiscoBaptiPentaGationalist. Yup, something you might have figured out about me by now! I grew up in a Congregationalist church; I was ordained under the tutelage of Gordon MacDonald, Warren Schuh and others at Grace Chapel, a Baptistic inter-denominational church; I was welcomed with open arms by the Pentecostals Ernie Tavilla introduced me to when I was president of Vision New England; and have been soul pastored by my amazing spiritual director, Br. David Vryhof, and the Episcopal Order of the Society of Saint John the Evangelist. I'm a religious mutt who has been influenced greatly by various streams of the pre- and post-Reformation Church. And, I have a growing appreciation for the variety of expressions in the body of Christ, ethnically, theologically, geographically, and in worship styles, forms of outreach, etc. I have loved and been captivated by the Church since an early age and continue to delight in her amazing diversity and importance yet today.

What I've discovered over the years as well is that Jesus loves the Church, his Bride, the body of Christ, the beloved people of God. And, if I love Jesus, as you know I do, I too need to love the Church he loves. In fact, he died for his Bride, and I too am to sacrifice my life in obedience to the same commitment. And so should you, my children, offspring of the previous generation of the Church and participants in developing, maintaining and sustaining the Church in your and for future generations. Regardless of your vocation, you too share the same calling to the Church. Without the Church we have no eternal family. The Church is filled with our true Brothers and Sisters, even more so than our earthly siblings. Our godly inheritance will forever be shared and enjoyed with those who have faith in the Triune God - Father, Son and Holy Spirit - and will be with us forever.

So, as we all await eternity with God, let me encourage you to be involved in the life of the Church today and all the days of your life. Some seasons you will be more active than others, as has been the case for your mother and me. But, in all ways and at all times, be sure to commit to God and your own families to invest time, talent and treasure in the Church. It's not perfect for sure, nor will it ever be. But, neither has been our own immediate family. Imperfect people just like us fill the pews of local churches, and it's incumbent upon us to do all we can to enrich the body of Christ with edifying words, attitudes and acts of love. That's been our family's goal since you were born – mostly at Grace Chapel, but also during our years at Park Street Church. And, in all my years at the helm of Vision New England and since then at Leadership Transformations, for each ministry I've led is focused on loving and serving God's Church. Let love be your guide and as you intentionally love and serve your own local church fellowship may you find much love and joy coming your way in return.

9
Take risks

Your dad took several large risks in his life. The first one was to say yes to following Jesus as a high school student in the midst of a time in our history (the early 1970's) when upheaval was occurring in our world and being a "Jesus freak" wasn't very popular. Another was applying to Northwestern College sight unseen, showing up on campus for the very first time as an incoming freshman having never been on campus (I didn't even know where Iowa was on the map. I thought I was heading geographically to Ohio!). A third risk was shifting from a single congregational ministry setting that we loved (Grace Chapel) to a regional ministry serving thousands of churches (Evangelistic Association of New England, which would become Vision New England in my tenure) and entering the world of non-profit organizations. But the biggest of all came when mom and I chose to venture into the entrepreneurial world of founding together the organization we serve today, Leadership Transformations, our greatest ministry legacy.

Each of these major risks came at a huge cost. And ended up becoming significant gifts from God. Each required letting go of the past and embracing the new and unknown of the future. Each meant we had to take a leap of faith and trust that God was in the middle of each decision. Each demanded much of us, but the return of investment was always richer than we ever could have asked, dreamed or imagined at the outset. That's the essential nature of risk-taking. But, without taking risks prayerfully and boldly and faithfully we are left with a life of inconsequential sameness. That has never been the life I wanted for myself, our family, or those with whom I have been called to lead and serve. Taking risks – especially for God – is what we are invited to do daily. Risk taking stretches our faith and leads us into concealed and yet to be discovered opportunities.

Never be afraid to take a risk. It takes courage to do so. And lots of faith in the unseen potential of what's ahead. But, without at least a handful of risks in life, your journey will be rather plain vanilla when it could be multi-colored, multi-faceted, multi-dimensional, and multi-enriched. You have both taken risks already – for example, Nate's risk of a big surgical procedure that would impact both legs; Bekah's risk of moving to Colorado – with consequences and potentiality unknown in advance. To take a risk is to believe in God's invisible presence and supernatural power to unleash a new way of being that's just around the corner awaiting your arrival. Taking prayerful, even calculated, risks is likened to embracing faith, without which your life will be boringly plain and ho-hum. Be bold and take a few big faith-filled risks, especially for the sake of Kingdom purposes God places upon your heart...they will undoubtedly transform your daily, with-God life and lead you into experiences that will shape and form you in Christ.

10
Faithful no matter what

I f you heard it from me once, you heard it several times: it's important to be a person of your word, faithful to God, one another and even to yourself, no matter what may come your way. This was drilled into me from early childhood as both your Papa and Nonna were people who exhibited faithfulness. I am forever indebted to them for modeling this for me, and teaching me that remaining faithful to God and one another was always the best way to go. Faithfulness mattered to them, even if it cost them to be so, either in reputation or in financial remuneration or in personal gain (or lack thereof). With faithfulness comes integrity, honesty, and authenticity, even when others are derailing and exhibiting the opposite. To be faithful means to be reliable, consistent, self-effacing, and free from the need to abandon ship or walk away angry.

We've always been a family faithful to the Red Sox and to all our hometown teams, faithful to the schools we attended and the churches we've been a part of. Faithful to our employers and the companies/organizations we serve. We've chosen to be faithful even to friends who turned their backs on us, and to institutions who we felt weren't living up to their integrity. Bottom line: faithfulness is a value we hold high no matter what may result. Making thoughtful decisions, sticking with our convictions, standing with others, remembering important dates in other people's lives. All of this is the fodder of faithfulness and all such decisions are what will bring you the greatest depth of satisfaction in every arena of life.

The world we live in today doesn't advocate for faithfulness. We live in a consumer driven society and the messages we hear continually surround taking care of you via self-promotion, provision and protection. Being faithful no matter what is a conscious decision of the will. So, when the going gets rough and the temptation is to walk away, please remember to pray and consider the consequences of turning your back on faithfulness. God is loving and faithful, and will always be there for you. Trust in his faithfulness and ask him to keep you faithful too...first and foremost to him, and then to his Word, his will for your life, and his way of being a Christ follower in this self-centered world. When you keep God's faithfulness central to your daily walk, trusting in his faithfulness when you feel led astray, you can indeed remain faithful, true to your word, your convictions, and mostly to your relationships, no matter what may come your way. For as long as I'm alive I will faithfully pray for your faithfulness.

What I'd like to add related to *Decisions Made:*

Key decisions made that positively formed and shaped my life:

_____

_____

_____

_____

_____

_____

_____

Ways in which I have discerned my own decision-making:

_____

_____

_____

_____

_____

_____

_____

Decisions that were more costly (emotionally, relationally, etc.) than others:

_____

_____

_____

_____

_____

_____

_____

One piece of advice as you make your own decisions:

_____

_____

_____

_____

_____

_____

_____

Additional thoughts:

_____

_____

_____

_____

_____

_____

_____

_____

_____

_____

_____

_____

_____

_____

_____

_____

_____

_____

_____

Section III:
Mistakes Regretted

"Where there is no revelation, people cast off restraint; but blessed is the one who heeds wisdom's instruction."

— Proverbs 29: 18

Something to ponder as you read this section: Which of your own regretted mistakes would you like to confess to the next generation in your family?

11

Holding too firm

Stubbornness seems to run in our family, and perhaps better stated, the entire human family. Needing to be right. Holding possessions too tightly. Wanting more than what I really need. Manipulating others to follow my way. Being closed minded, opinionated and judgmental. Unwilling to admit when I'm wrong or budge on a strongly held conviction. All of these are evidences of a stubborn heart, and unfortunately you've seen all of this in one way or another as you've observed my life. I'm not at all proud of how stubborn I've been over the years. As I've gotten older, I can see with greater clarity the ripple affects of stubbornness. And, when any of this occurs it makes for a stern approach and a rather stinky life! No one responds well to stubbornness.

One of the net negative affects of stubbornness is that it can be contagiously transferred to others. Yes, and for that I apologize. I've contributed to your stubbornness and I regret that deeply. It seems to travel the family lineage and when it does so it can cause ripple effects in the hearts of those you know the best and love the most. I've had my share of holding too firmly to my possessions, my attitudinal positions, and my relationships, and for that I am sorry. I've had my opinions about what is best for you and even with all the best intentions as your father to encourage you toward a strong sense of independence and healthy interdependence, I've come across promoting something more akin to co-dependence. Please forgive me. It's not at all healthy for me to hold too firm of a grip on you or your attempts at maturing on your own.

What I much prefer is a life of open-handedness, open-heartedness, and open-mindedness. And not just mildly so, but fully and abundantly. Often when I teach on the Christian life I will extend my arms out fully as an expression of one's desire for the wholeness of God rather than just a portion of God. Jesus died on the cross and his outstretched arms of love are the symbol of an open-hearted life. He gave fully of himself, he was open and available to all, and he loved others indiscriminately. That's the kind of life I want to live, but so often that intention was thwarted by my propensity to control, manipulate, or hold too firmly. God's call on our lives is to empty ourselves of ourselves, be filled up with God and his Word, and live open-handedly among others. May you, my children, be freed from your own stubbornness and live abundantly with God, graciously detached from any and all of your unholy attachments.

12

Letting the sun go down on my anger

There are few things worse relationally than ending a day with anger in your heart. As a family, we sought to avoid this at all costs, especially when you were children. Both of you were pretty sweet about making amends at the end of the day and not allowing bad feelings to worsen overnight. I remember with fondness and regularity, closing Bekah's door after our bedtime routines, turning off the light and then hearing her gentle voice cry out, "I'm sorry if I was bad or crabby today" and our assuring her, "Thanks, Bek, love you honey...sleep sweet." And her final words, "Ok, thanks...love you," and our final reassuring "Love you too." Tender memories indeed.

But, if I'm honest with you, there were indeed days that I wasn't as humble hearted (you probably could attest to that yourself). After full days of ministry and home life, there were more days than I care to admit that ended in frustration, impatience, and even anger. And, what I regret the most is that you or Mom caught the brunt end of my frustrations – never my intention or desire, but in the emotion of the moment you were there as recipients. This happens in far too many homes today – it doesn't excuse it, but it does help to explain the reality of family life. The Bible is pretty clear about this one, "Don't let the sun go down on your anger" (Eph. 4:26). And the reason is evident: when we finish our day in a sour state, we open the door for the enemy of our soul to wreak havoc on our hearts and minds and relationships overnight. Not a pretty picture for anyone affected (or should I say infected?).

Remember your childlike heart in this regard, and with gentleness and grace end your days well, and as much as possible without a hint of anger toward anyone and even toward yourself. It's never worth it to let anger fester in your heart, regardless of the time of day. There's always time to make it right, but be careful not to fan the flame of discontent by choosing the wrong time (i.e. when exhaustion can actually lead to additional conflict) or way of doing so (i.e. with a selfish motive). Whenever the devil is given room to run rampant in your heart he will trip you up, tempt you down, and turn you upside down and inside out with turmoil that will pull you out of sorts and out of touch with those you love the most...aargh, avoid letting the sun go down on your anger at all costs.

13

Festering betrayal eating away my soul

My life overall has been pretty free of relational disaster. But, I can point to a small handful of significant betrayals. Each time it emerged was a complete surprise, as the betrayal came from unlikely sources. However, there were two in particular that scarred my heart and threw me off in a major way. One came from a ministry colleague and the other from a long-time friendship. Apparently I had done something which triggered their frustration and ultimately their betrayal. Both times they were revealed circuitously and indirectly, which added to the hurt and disappointment. When I attempted reconciliation there was immediate defensiveness on one occasion and absolute silence on the other. Both have been huge disappointments to swallow.

When I learned of the betrayals I immediately jumped in to try and rectify the situation and seek to understand what happened. But, each time the persons involved refused to talk about it with me. Instead, I was turned away with distant coldness. One relationship was eventually healed (even though the collegiality today is somewhat skewed as a result); the other has yet to be resolved. Given my personality, and my desire for closure on all conflicts large or small, these two betrayals ate away at my heart and negatively affected my work, my spiritual life, and my relationships for months thereafter. Given the lack of resolution, and the time involved in seeking some form of meaningful restitution, I held onto the pain and heartache longer than I should have for a number of reasons, none of which were justifiable. Just writing about it now, years later, evokes the pain of both situations.

So, my fatherly advice on this issue is if and when this happens to you, do what you can to humbly seek resolution. Listen intently to the concerns raised. Confess your sin as needed. Strive for peace and resolution. Forgive and then forgive again (even though you may or may not forget). Learn from your mistakes. Develop relational health and trust all over again. Avoid hurting others as much as you're able to do so, and be open to receiving feedback about how you're coming across to others. And, remember that relationships are one of life's best gifts, and yet in the heart and mind of others they may in fact be rather fickle. Betrayals may be hard to shake off, must be prayed through, talked out, and hopefully worked out with grace, mercy, empathy and compassion. Try not to let them eat away at your soul.

14

Holding back
unconfessed sin

When I first heard the phrase "we are as sick as our secrets" I bristled. This seemed like such a harsh comment, as if holding back from confession of whatever secret sin we found impossible to voice would result in our sickness. But, upon reflection, I have since realized the poignancy of this principle. Indeed, our deeply held secrets are the place where the enemy of our soul loves to lurk and linger as permanently as possible, and ultimately wreak havoc on our mind, heart, soul, and even our health. The devil knows that if he's successful in convincing us that we don't have to confess every single sin we commit, he's assured of our sickness of soul.

The value of confessing our sins, first to God and then to a trusted confidante or to the one we've offended, is what leads us into freedom and joy. The truth about ourselves – even the ugly truth – will always set us free. That's what confession means: speak the truth, give voice to and confess it, and then enter the process of giving and receiving forgiveness and reconciliation. Sin – our disobedience to God, another and even to ourselves – is what keeps us at a distance from all who are affected. In fact, our sin can even impact those not directly involved, as the ripple effects of our sinfulness can reach beyond and around us like a cancerous tumor affects one's whole body. Most significantly, it can keep us from becoming all that God intends and hinders our ability to draw close to God, the One to Whom we must confess in the first place.

When you are aware of your sin, it's always best to confess it as quickly as possible. If your sin is against God directly, be sure to express your sorrow and your desire for his grace, mercy and forgiveness. Harder still, if it's toward another person in whom you interact face to face, come clean and articulate as best as possible how saddened you are by your omission or commission of word, thought or deed toward them, and ask for their forgiveness. Even deeper to navigate is what you do to yourself, choosing to entertain shame and blame that appear to be impossible to overcome, and yet bring out the deepest part of you that needs healing, grace, forgiveness and reconciliation. Confession of one's sin is by far one of the most difficult admissions of all, without which sickness of heart, soul, mind, and even our bodies can result. For indeed, we are as sick as our secrets – so, choose health! Choose confession! Choose truth! Choose forgiveness! Choose joy!

15
Didn't play enough

Having a strong work ethic was drilled into me from an early age. Your Papa, my dad, worked hard each day. He'd put in a full day in the office and then come home to attend to our needs, either working out in the garden, fixing something we had broken, paying the bills, tinkering in the basement, you name it, Papa could do it. Even though I'm more the "thinkerer" than "tinkerer" (one of Papa's expressions) I too have done my best to provide for my family, knowing that hard work was the means to that end. And, my early mentors were hard workers who didn't play much either, so neither did they encourage play for us as their underlings. You've already shown your employers what hard work looks like too, and for that I am very proud of you. Your work ethic matters, just like your work matters – to God, your family, and all you serve. You've learned that well and we Macchia's work hard at every job put in front of us. That's a good thing.

But the sad reality for me is that I worked disproportionately to play. I'm the first to admit that the "to do" list or the "honey do" list preoccupied me so much that the last thing to ever appear on any priority list was "play"! I always knew of its importance, and could stand up in front of a crowd or write an article that espoused its absolute essential significance. But the strong words I articulated were not followed up by action. And yet, whenever I do play, it's nothing short of life-giving, even though my form of "play" was different from many of my peers (i.e. individual sports like biking or tennis; and hobbies like photography, reading, hiking, traveling, and being near water of any kind were more of my preference). What I have yet to get right and what I regret in this regard is within the realm of exercise. There is some kind of deep aversion within me to regular care of my physical body, as in the pummeling of my body for rigorous purposes. Diet and nutrition, sleep and medical care, were all fine. But I never hit stride in regular exercise. As a result, you didn't see in me a good role model for you to follow.

I regret not modeling "play" better for you so that you too could embrace it as a necessary part of life. I so wish I had embraced early on the principles of 8: 8 hours of productive work, 8 hours of productive play, and 8 hours of productive rest each day. My life would have been so different. So, instead of remorse over what could or should have been, I simply want to encourage you to discover the places, people, and activities that give you life in the out-of-the-ordinary way that play alone can provide. I trust that you'll find exercise routines that keep your mind sharp and your body fit; that you'll embrace hobbies that can be sources of great joy for your soul and relationships; and that you'll simply choose to play more and not always work - for the sake of your wholeness of character, the quality of your relationships, and the abundance of your life! Play more, play smart, play today!

What I'd like to add related to *Mistakes Regretted*:

Major (and minor) mistakes that I personally regret:

_____

_____

_____

_____

_____

_____

_____

Ways I could have avoided making these mistakes:

_____

_____

_____

_____

_____

_____

_____

Redemptive values instilled in my heart as a result of my mistakes:

_____

_____

_____

_____

_____

_____

_____

One piece of advice as you will inevitably make mistakes you will regret:

_____

_____

_____

_____

_____

_____

_____

Additional thoughts:

Section IV:
Relationships Enjoyed

"As iron sharpens iron, so one person sharpens another."

— Proverbs 27: 17

Something to ponder as you read this section: Which of your own primary relationships would you like to be highlighted for the next generation in your family?

16

Family, our imperfect loved ones

If you haven't noticed already, our family is not perfect...not even close to being perfect. In fact, we're fundamentally kinda messed up - but oh so normal. What you experienced in our household was the best we could provide for you given our own capabilities, even though our provision was often incomplete and imperfect at its core. There's no such thing as a perfect family, even when other families may give you that impression. If you had always hoped for something different or more or better or another variation of expectation for us, I'm sorry to say you'd be disappointed. Our family is just like every other family, but the particulars of our imperfections are uniquely ours. Not necessarily something to treasure or brag about (even though there is a ton of positives to brag about!), but instead a reality to embrace: our family is imperfect.

But, what our family has done for you and one another is consistent: we have loved as we best know how to love. And even that leads to lots of variation, because you know extended family members of ours who love sacrificially and humbly, and you know other family members of ours who only know how to love manipulatively and grievously. The former are considered life givers, and the latter are the opposite: narcissistic life killers. One kind of lover shows interest in you and wants the best for you while the other loves you only and conditionally for their own well-being. The true lover is available, attentive, prayerful, listening, empathic, while the self-consumed lover is egotistical, unkind, unavailable, and really kind of sick. Unfortunately our extended family has their share of the latter, much to our chagrin. The genuine lovers know they are imperfect, live within that reality, and consistently give of themselves even in their imperfect way. Those are my kind of people, and yours too.

So what's to be your response? To love as you best know how to love! And, my prayer is that your love will be the kind that considers others more important than yourself, looks out for another's best interests, always defends one another no matter what, and will be the kind of lover that loves by intentionally bringing out the best in all: embodying heartfelt grace, mercy, kindness, gentleness, patience, and forgiveness. Your mother and I have sought to do this for you each day, and although we have failed more times than we care to acknowledge, our hope has been that we've modeled enough of the good stuff of love for you to practice and express it better than most. Your love will often be imperfect, but with God reigning in your heart and mind, you will do well in offering your form of love to each member of our and your future family. Go for it!

17

Lifelong, life-giving friendships

The richness of my life can be found in my friendships, second only to our relationships as a family. When you someday scatter my remains over the Atlantic Ocean along Eastern Point in Gloucester (don't forget!), one thing you can say of me: he had many lifelong, life-giving friendships. I attribute this to my childhood desire for a brother, who never came (no offense meant toward two absolutely amazing sisters!). So, as the years progressed I purposed to have brothers from other mothers, and God saw fit to answer my simple boyhood prayer through the lives of my friends. Most of them were male, but I also enjoyed many special friendships with women too. And, interestingly, they came from the Christian community I experienced first at college, and then later in church, and in my various ministry contexts.

Their names would all be recognizable to you, as you've been included over the years in the quality of these lives and their families. What's even more descriptive of them is the kind of friends they were: having attentively listening ears, embodying prayerfully gracious lives, engaging in fun-loving and life-giving experiences, becoming available during times of crisis, being there to offer words of hope and comfort and peace, sharing in the joys, trials, accomplishments and even the heartaches of life. True friends are hard to come by, but as my mom often said "If you want a friend, be a friend" and I did everything possible to be the best friend I could become for each who showed affection and appreciation for me. As a result, I often feel like the richest man alive, given both the quantity and quality of my friendships.

Your life will be all the richer too, as you proactively cultivate your own set of friendships. You have both experienced friendships great and hard, and you know the joy and challenge that accompanies this pursuit. But, I can assure you at my age that there is nothing beyond family more important than the gift of friendship. And a gift it is indeed, one that is to be treasured, trusted, and tried throughout your life. You have a fundamental choice ahead of you each day: will you be for another the kind of friend you so desire for yourself? If so, then practice the Golden Rule daily: do unto others what you want done to you. And, love your friends as you love yourself – for all the days of your life. Your truest friends will stay the course and love you to life in all its abundance. I can attest to that myself and I pray you will too.

18

Those who mentor me

One of my ministry mentors once said to me "someday you'll outgrow your need for a mentor" and of all his incredibly insightful sayings, this is his most shortsighted one. Even if I'm not in more formal mentoring relationships, I hope to always be open to the wisdom of those who have gone before me in life. For there will always be people around me who have something to offer those who are at least a handful of years ahead of me from whom I can glean. Even now I have a spiritual director with whom I meet monthly, and have done so for more than two decades. Having David Vryhof in my life has been huge for my spiritual development and I'm forever grateful. In addition, I am currently searching for a CEO coach to learn from as I transition out of my leadership role at LTI over this next decade. I trust both Mom and I have exemplified this relational priority before you. How we thank God for our mentors who have influenced us in many significant ways personally, professionally, spiritually, and interpersonally.

My first mentor was your "Uncle" Rich, the man who led me into my personal relationship with Jesus as Lord and Savior when I was a junior in high school. Remarkably, we've kept in touch with each other for more than 40 years and our relationship continues to strengthen with every new season of life. Rich has mentored me in my faith, in my marriage, in my ministry, and in my daily life. He's been there for me in good times of celebration (conducting our wedding ceremony, speaking at my ordination) and in hard times of disappointment and difficulty. His mentorship has been biblically-based, relationally-strong, and personally-focused. His words have often been comforting, but also challenging, and even convicting at times. He has entered into my story and sought my redemption and renewal whenever possible.

You too will need at least one and hopefully more mentors in your life. You've already had coaches, pastors, bosses, and older, wiser friends who have served you in this capacity. As you grow into your thirties and beyond, the need for mentors will not diminish. Mentors reinforce and augment what we as your parents have sought to offer to you: the wisdom of the ages. Those who are good mentors will lead you down paths of righteousness, purity, humility, patience, and grace. They will pray for you, serve your best interests and needs, and provide a listening ear and time-tested wisdom for the various roles, responsibilities, and rhythms of your life. They will be there when you reach goals and accomplishments, and when you fall down, need a hug, a listening ear, a word of perspective, or simply a shoulder to cry on. Mainly, they will love you and offer the gift of presence when you need it most. Look for trusted mentors and then entrust them with all the major and even the minor aspects of your life.

19

Those I disciple and coach

Ithank God for the privilege of coming alongside others who are younger in faith, in ministry, and in life, and serve as their discipler, mentor, coach, counselor, confidante, and/or spiritual director. Each role is discipleship focused, for whenever I'm in such a relationship I know that my number one responsibility is to help another get closer to Jesus. And in that regard, to aid them in their ability to trust in the Lord with their whole heart, soul, mind and strength. As a disciple of Jesus myself, I find it pure joy to serve those younger than me as an older, wiser disciple who has sought to incline my life in Jesus' direction, practicing for many years how to distinguish his voice among the cacophony, having followed him for many more years than the one I'm discipling.

Thankfully, my ministry has allowed me the opportunity to serve in this capacity many times. When we served at Grace Chapel, I was in a discipling relationship with junior high students, volunteer staff members, young marrieds, and others who were a part of our ministry. Since then, at Vision New England and now at Leadership Transformations and the Pierce Center at Gordon-Conwell Theological Seminary, I'm rich with such relationships. Although appearing to be lopsided in the direction of the disciple, I'm also the recipient of the blessings that come with this tender relationship. As a discipler, I have the privilege of listening attentively to the stories of hope and hurt that fill a life. I also have the joy of praying with them, advising, advocating, and affirming God's handiwork in their life. It's awesome and amazing.

As you mature in your own faith and life, I want to challenge you to offer your wisdom to those with whom you too can disciple. You don't need to have all the answers, just a listening ear and a humble, teachable heart. In these relationships, you are learning how to trust God to be the One who does all the transformational discipleship work in the heart and life of another. Don't take yourself so seriously that you begin to think instead that it's you doing all the work! A big part of this role is learning how to entrust the life and story of another into the loving, gentle, gracious hands of God. Then, by opening his Word, the Scriptures, and leaning on his Spirit in prayer, you and your disciple are together growing in intimacy with the God of the universe who loves both of you with an infinite, matchless love. It's when you see God at work in the heart of another that brings about the deepest of all satisfaction. And then all you can say is "Wow, God! Thanks for your deep work in each of our lives!"

20

Those I serve in Jesus' name

For nearly forty years, your mom and I have been serving others in Jesus' name. It's hard to believe that four decades ago I sensed the call to ministry and said a hearty yes to God's invitation! And ever since then our lives have been fully devoted to building up the saints for the work of ministry in, to and for this world. For us, the sphere of ministry has included children, youth, young marrieds, families, leaders, the saved and the unsaved, the marginalized and the inner circle, sinners and saints alike. I've had the privilege of serving people of various vocations, ethnicities, and socio-economic backgrounds. The diversity has been remarkable, but the needs are universal. Soul care for all is and has always been my number one priority.

The relationships I've had with those I've served have varied, from the most difficult to the most lovable, from the least and the lost and the left behind to the highest and the saved and the most active and productive of all. I've had the delight of coming alongside neighbors like Richard and Joan, who followed Gramma Mae in the house next to ours, and befriended us and you as we served them in ways we most naturally could offer. We were invited to be a part of the 100th birthday celebration of Gramma Mae, Nate worked part time for Richard, and I was asked to speak at Richard's funeral. All of our connections were birthed out of service in Jesus' name, whether through taking trash out for Gramma Mae, or shoveling her walkway. In trimming their bushes or in lengthy conversation, the service was offered out of love and affection for them as people made in the image of the Creator who placed his unique stamp on their lives. God brought our lives together and serving them was always a joy.

However, serving others in Jesus' name isn't always joy-filled. At times it's tiresome, disappointing, and even hurtful to body, mind and/or spirit. Serving others comes at a cost, the high cost of self-denial, and cross-like sacrifice. Yes, serving others even includes suffering, something we don't like to talk much about and do everything possible to avoid. But, when serving others in Jesus' name is costly, it's also the most rewarding. Jesus suffered and died out of service to his followers. He didn't just wash their dirty feet, he stretched out his arms of love and suffered the most painful death of all – on the cross and out of love and service to all who would call upon his name and be saved. I hereby call you to such service, my children, service that will cost you your very lives in love and obedience to Jesus. But, service like this is the best we have to offer to the Best Who Offered Himself so that we can live and love and serve in his Name. All to Jesus, all for Jesus, and all in Jesus - the only way to live is to serve others, coming from your abiding with Jesus every single day. Go for it, ok? I'll cheer you on forever!

What I'd like to add related to *Relationships Enjoyed:*

Most important relationships in my life include:

_____

_____

_____

_____

_____

_____

_____

_____

Ways in which these key relationships were deepened and enhanced:

_____

_____

_____

_____

_____

_____

_____

Relational priorities to uphold as well as best ways to maintain healthy relationships:

_____

_____

_____

_____

_____

_____

_____

_____

One piece of advice as you foster your own relationships:

_____

_____

_____

_____

_____

_____

_____

_____

Additional thoughts:

_____

_____

_____

_____

_____

_____

_____

_____

_____

_____

_____

_____

_____

_____

_____

_____

_____

_____

_____

Section V: Words Spoken

"Above all else, guard your heart, for everything you do flows from it."

— Proverbs 4: 23

Something to ponder as you read this section: Which of your own key words would you like to impress upon the next generation in your family?

21
Encouragement

We are fortunate to live so close to the Boston Marathon, the premier 26.2 mile annual road race that's known worldwide. We've taken you to a few of these over the years, watching and cheering on friends who have participated (never was an aspiration of mine!). Nate and I even had the unique privilege of getting great seats at the Finish Line from a generous businessman in Boston. What I love about marathons from the sidelines are the water stations every mile or so where runners are handed a cup of cold water to either consume or pour out on their head, face or chest. That cup of cold water is what sustains them in the race and both literally and figuratively encourages them to continue to run to the finish line. That's by far my favorite analogy for one of my all-time favorite words: encouragement.

You know people who have faithfully stood along the sidelines of your life, and even ran beside you, and are filled to overflowing with encouragement. It oozes from the pores of their soul. Those who immediately come to mind were teachers you had in elementary school, small group leaders you had at church, family friends who embraced you as their own. And you've had your share, as I have, of those who do the opposite – even choosing not to be there and worse yet holding back the cup of cold water as if to punish or shame or humiliate you as they watch you run on your own. To encourage another, however, is to impart courage, inspire hope, increase confidence and instill endurance into your heart so that no matter what hills you may climb or turbulence you may experience or potholes you may encounter, you know you're supported and encouraged by another.

Encouragement comes in various forms: a kind word, a gentle touch, a thoughtful prayer, a helpful deed, a generous gift, a loving surprise, and a heart-warming story. It even comes as a truthful correction or a challenge to grow. The delivery of encouragement is always a welcome relief for those engaged fully in the marathon of life. Bekah, you do this so well and so naturally – you are an encouragement to so many simply by your smile and your willing heart to love and serve. So let me encourage you both to encourage others and to do so daily. All of us not only need several hugs per day, we also need lots of encouragement. No one is exempt from this need, even though others may stiffen at the thought. Encouragement is the way of love and to avoid this is to ignore an incredible opportunity to offer a cup of cold water in Jesus' name. May you always be generous in encouragement.

22
Exhortation ABC's

An active companion to encouragement is exhortation. I didn't realize I had the spiritual gift of exhortation until a colleague of mine pointed it out to me. Angela said very directly, "it's obvious you exhort another by wanting the best to emerge from within them, urging others to lean fully into the next thing God has for them." And I resonated deeply with that very insightful comment about your dad: I truly do love urging others to greater depth in their relationship with God, heightened awareness of themselves, and increased vitality in their service to others. Many have received this gift with gratitude, while others (even you two at times!) have bristled under the weight of such challenges. But, when exercised in the Spirit, it truly does evoke powerful encounters with God and incredible growth in godliness for the individual.

What I've tried to remember about exhortation is that it can't be delivered without first earning the right to say a challenging word. I call it the "ABC's" of relationships: first you need to affirm (state clearly and frequently how much you value the person and how their gifts, talents and simply their presence means to you); second, you need to build up that person (investing time and energy in the relationship, even giving of yourself so that others know you care and want the very best for them); so that thirdly you can challenge another (offering words that will exhort them to consider a new way of thinking, being or acting toward all of life's situations). Affirm – Build – Challenge, the ABC's of healthy relationships, and always in that order.

Even though I acknowledge this gift of exhortation as one that I possess, I still want to urge you toward the essence of exhortation for yourself. What I mean is, that whenever possible, to look at life's highs and lows as invitations from God for you to grow and mature in trusting the Lord amidst every challenge he allows to come your way. Be exhorted first of all by our loving God who wants to be continually inviting you into the trusting way, but also by others like your dad who love you up to the moon and back again and want nothing more than the very best for you! And then as you come alongside others in life's never-ending journey, may you too serve another by bringing out their very best and the fullest expression of their true personhood. It's one of the best ways we can love and serve others as Jesus would have us do. He wants us to be fully alive for sure. Exhortation is a great gift to offer when it's genuinely shared out of a heart of love. Affirm, build, challenge, and exhort in Jesus' name!

23

Blessing and joy

Two of my favorite words are "blessing" and "joy" – two words that describe how I feel about both of you, my dearly loved offspring, a blessing and a joy to my heart. Even as I write this series of reflections for you I find myself in an extended season of concluding emails and notes with the valediction, "Blessings and Joy in Christ Alone." They are symbolic of the state of my soul and the gratitude of my heart. There's something very powerful to me about those two words, especially when offered to another. When we are wishing both blessings and joys to be extended to a friend or loved one, we are hoping for the goodness of God to be poured out upon their hearts and lives. Blessings that come from the hand of God, and joys that accompany them, are profound gifts of delight for the heart, mind and soul of another.

You have received so many blessings and joys in your life, and you've generously offered the same to others who have crossed your path. I've witnessed this over and over again. Our family has been richly blessed by God. We are some of the most fortunate, and I hope you've seen in us a desire to be a blessing to others in return. You've acquired this ability and I celebrate it in you. Nate's obvious color-blindness toward those of different skin color when he was young. Or, his willingness to accept another even with their accompanying handicap and befriend the disabled out of genuine love. Bekah's empathy for the underdog, the forgotten, or the lonely. And, her continual desire to take on challenging relationships even when they turned against her maliciously. Both of you have been an inspiration to your mother and me, when at times we have been hurt and the last thing we want to give our offender is a blessing and a joy.

To live purposefully with an earnest desire to bless another is to embody the Spirit of Jesus, who blessed every person who entered his sphere of influence. Sometimes the blessings came as words of healing grace, while other times the blessings were delivered as prayers, parables, or practical advice. Some of the blessings were tangible, but the best were the ones that changed the heart. To be in the presence of Jesus was enough to create joy in the hearts of the repentant, the responsive, and even the reticent. So, let me bless you with the joy of knowing Jesus, free you up to be a blessing to others, so that your joy may increase and multiply as you radiate the love of Jesus to all who cross your path today and always. Deliver blessings and joys and you'll lessen the temptation to want them only for yourself.

24

Prayers

One of the most misspoken phrases is "I'll pray for you" or "You are in my prayers" when in fact that's more often our Christianese for the more accurate saying, "I'm thinking of you" or "You are often thought about." And yet one of the best gifts you can offer to another is to simply and seriously offer prayers in their behalf. This is so that when you find yourself saying "I'll pray for you" you are in fact bringing him/her before the Lord either in your prayer closet or merely praying as you go throughout your day. Prayers offered for others, and even for yourself, are the dialogue we can have with the God of the universe who has nothing but affection for you and for those you bring to him in prayer.

A beautiful analogy for offering our intercessory prayers for one another was first shared with me by Brother Geoffrey at the Society of Saint John the Evangelist. He wrote and spoke about our prayers using the biblical image of the "Breastplate of Aaron," the man we know was called by God to be the prayer warrior for Moses (holding up Moses' arms as he prayed). The image of a breastplate, in Aaron's case filled with jewels representing the twelve tribes of Israel, is stunning to behold. Imagine Aaron wearing this into the "holy of holies," prayerfully entering that awe-inspiring space with all of the people of God brought before the Lord as signified by each gemstone. His point was that all we're asked to do is to bring others before God's throne of grace and by delivering them into God's merciful hands we are praying for their protection and peace. Nothing more complicated than that, and with words optional, we simply show up with our friends on our hearts and hand them over to God.

Prayers are not to be taken for granted or held less than holy, no matter what the concern may be. So, my beloved ones, I implore you to be people of prayer - simply and sacredly offering any and all of your praises, petitions and pleas before the God of love. When you can entrust all of your prayers into his faithful hands, it's like taking a burdensome backpack off your shoulders and laying every concern at his feet. In fact, that's exactly what God wants you to do: humbly offer your prayers and release your concerns, knowing that the God of all knowledge, power, peace, and presence has everything under his control. He will do or not do according to his good pleasure. By offering our prayers and the people of our prayers before the living God we can enter and exit his particular presence with assurance that he hears all of our prayers and will answer them according to his good and perfect will. Will you entrust your prayers to God and will you faithfully deliver those with whom you pray into his grace-filled hands? May it be so, my beloved. Amen.

25

Abundant life

Oh to live an abundant life! Not in the ways of the world…wealth of possessions, physical health and strength, control and power over others. But instead in the ways of God: abundance of love, joy, peace, patience, kindness, goodness, faithfulness, gentleness and self-control. Yes, abundant in the fruit of the Spirit, which is the evidence of God at work instilling and imparting his very self into you his cherished and highly adored child. In order to live abundantly, we need to learn how to acquire such abundance, and that only comes from God's Spirit, the One who delivers the fullness of God into the heart and life of the ones he lovingly and providently created as his own. This comes as we remain in God, steadfastly earnest in our pursuit of God, keeping our eyes fixed on Christ and abiding in his love. You are offered the abundant life and as your dad I hope you accept the offer and remain there all the days of your life!

None of the nine lovely fruit of the Spirit can be acquired by human agility, exertion or aptitude. None of them can be thought into existence or willed into practice. The only way one can obtain the fruit is by remaining available to receive the fruit from God. Receive-ability is what's essential. How receivable do we generally find ourselves, when in this world we are continually challenged to do life on our own strength, ability and power. We're invigorated by the options before us and catapulted into self-protection and self-empowerment, self-willed to take care of that which comes our way or to seek out that which will somehow create a (false) sense of security about the here and now of our daily experience. We want, crave, strive, compete, and then seek to control our own destiny, rather than be open and available to God.

I've striven enough to share point blank with you: it ain't worth it! When life is all about what I can gain by manipulating my way through each and every experience and relationship, then I'm for sure working toward my own agenda regardless of others. When instead I open myself up to fully receive that which God delights to hand to me, the good, the bad, and the ugly, I can live in freedom without all the worldly entrapments that have since occupied and preoccupied my mind and will. When I'm free to receive and give in the power of the Spirit then I'm living abundantly. In that posture I remain available for God to live in, through and all around me. And that's my prayer for you, my loved ones…that you too would be open to receive all that God wills for you to have, enjoying or enduring whatever comes your way. Most of all, that by receiving the gifts of God's Spirit you will share the abundance of the fruitful life in the Spirit of God and for all whom you encounter on planet earth.

What I'd like to add related to *Words Spoken:*

Words that have defined my daily life and marked my person-hood:

_____

_____

_____

_____

_____

_____

_____

Words that were spoken to me and about me that were hard to hear:

_____

_____

_____

_____

_____

_____

_____

Words I have valued the most – hearing and speaking them as life-givers:

_____

_____

_____

_____

_____

_____

_____

One piece of advice as you learn how best to communicate to others:

_____

_____

_____

_____

_____

_____

_____

Additional thoughts:

Section VI
Pilgrimages Traveled

"In their hearts humans plan their course, but the Lord establishes their steps."

— Proverbs 16:9

Something to ponder as you read this section: Which of your own pilgrimages would you like to recount with the next generation in your family?

26
Eastern European missions

For the past decade I've had the privilege of traveling with Rick Anderson to Eastern Europe for shared mission adventures, which have included stops before or after at various countries in Europe. The first two years we went to Latvia, serving with our friend Chuck Kelley and Bridge Builders International, speaking and interacting with local pastors and leaders. For the past eight years we have traveled to Moldova, the poorest country in Eastern Europe, a former Soviet Union/Russia-occupied country landlocked between Romania and the Ukraine. We have been warmly welcomed by all the Eastern Europeans we've met along the way, finding some distinct kinship with my own European and Italian roots.

Not only have I enjoyed traveling with my dear friend and colleague, but I've discovered within me what your mom loves to describe as my "wonder lust" – my longing for new adventures in uncharted territories. It's true. She's right. I do love to travel, especially with a purpose to attend to and then play thereafter. It's a good rhythm! The Moldovans have become very special to us, especially Vitalie Fedula, his wife Larisa and their only daughter Corina. Their gracious, generous and loving hospitality has been a wonderful joy. We've served with them in their amazing church, Jesus Savior Church, in the capital city of Chisinau. This church has been in partnership with Grace Chapel for more than thirty years, and we go as emissaries of the church and of LTI. We've preached, taught, and interacted with their leaders, mostly focused on developing the young adult leadership in the church. These dear ones hold a special place in my heart.

I share all of this with you to encourage you to prayerfully consider where in our wider world you can invest time, energy and financial resources to help those less fortunate than you. I'm confident you will discover the joy of serving others, noting how graciously God will provide for you in return, especially through the love and affection you receive from each people group you come alongside. Having a mission heart is something that pleases God and it's what I hope you will cultivate too. You've both had your short-term mission experiences when you were in high school, traveling with a team of fellow servants. Recall these trips with fondness, reminisce about the significance they had for you at that season of life, and prayerfully consider how to establish this priority, as you both have so much to offer through your gifts and abilities. I'm confident that a mission mindset and accompanying lifestyle will add immeasurable meaning to your life.

27
Italy the beautiful

Over the past decade or more I've purposed to see a new country each year. I haven't always hit that goal, but when I turned 50 I made this a particular focus. As a result, either with your mom or with Rick, I've seen many of the European countries, and Kenya in the continent of Africa. There's so much of the world yet to see and my bucket list is bulging with travel desires! But, of all the places we've visited, my heart leaps with delight when I'm in Italy. I've only been there three times, but each visit unlocks something deep within me that I love to see come alive. I'm sure it has to do with our family heritage, but there's something extra special about the land and the people of Italy. There is beauty around every corner and I come alive in that special land.

We've seen many of the major cities, Rome, Florence, Venice, as well as many ancient hilltop towns, such as Orvieto and Assisi, my favorite places in all of Italy. We've been there on pilgrimage with others, and we've been there just the two of us. Mom's favorite is the region of Tuscany, especially Chianti, where we stayed for our 30th anniversary. We also liked seeing the leaning tower of Pisa, and traverse the hillside communities of the Cinque Terre region along the coastline. Rome was a bit overwhelming but the piazzas are romantic, the churches are spectacular, the Vatican and St. Peter's Square are awesome. We are already looking forward to our next visit when we can travel east of Rome to Chieti, where the Macchia's are from, and then to southern Italy, along the coast and inland to as many southern communities as possible.

I hope to someday take our family to Italy. It would be such fun to travel together and explore one of the most beautiful countries of the world. But, in the meantime, I hope you can do as much international travel as you can afford. It might mean you do so before you have children, or waiting as we did until your children have grown up and most of your major expenses, such as providing for their college education, are behind you. Either way, seeing other parts of the world reminds you of the vastness of this world, the uniqueness of each land, culture and ethnicity, the disparities that separate us and the similarities that should unite us. Having a God-size view of the world will help you sift and sort through the challenges of understanding why and how people are so distinct from us and yet how beautiful those differences can be when seen through the lens of the cultural setting from which they emerge worldwide.

28
New adventures await

T he United States of America is filled with wonderful places to visit. We tried to take you to as many states as possible while you were growing up. We have many special memories of our travels to the Midwest (Iowa, South Dakota, Minnesota, Wisconsin), California, the Pacific Northwest (Oregon and Washington), Florida, Washington DC, New York (and NYC), over the border into Canada, and of course all of the six New England states. Each of our annual vacations took us somewhere new. Mom and I were purposeful in our vacation planning, saving our limited resources, and making sure the times were memorable for all of us. We did well as a ministry family, and whether it was flying to our destination or packing up the minivan (remember the Plymouth Voyager with wood paneling, and a vast interior space to enjoy during longer trips?), we made it safely to each of our vacation destinations.

By far the most time we spent on vacation as a family was on Cape Cod. Your Nonna and Papa were generous to allow us to use the 60-foot mobile home the Macchia family owned at Airline Mobile Home Park in South Dennis MA. You loved swimming in the pool, riding your bikes, playing with new friends, and going with us to Cold Storage Beach in East Dennis. We were at that beach countless times, walking the jetty, collecting shells during low tide, building sand castles, swimming in the ocean, and simply enjoying the sunshine and warmth of a summer day on the Cape. Rainy days were nasty, and worse yet were days when one of you (mostly Nate!) would get sick and require a visit to the local doctor's office. But, all in all, we loved our adventures on the Cape – the new ones as well as the tried and true ones. And, with places like Chatham, Orleans, Hyannis and P-Town to explore, there was always someplace fun to visit.

During your college years those trips slowed down considerably as you were getting summer jobs, and then post-college you set out on your own and took vacations during times that fit your personal schedules. We always tried to instill within you the importance of taking the vacation time allotted to you, since the opportunity to rest will only come when you take the time for slowing down and enjoying places to see that are different from your normal everyday routine. We knew that new adventures awaited us each time we'd travel to a new state and we took full advantage of that each summer, and during many of your school vacation weeks. Don't forget to do so each year for the rest of your life. Work will always be there, so enjoy time with friends and family in creative, life-giving, travel adventures. Where will you head next?

29

Life giving water and seasonal bounty

Pilgrimage doesn't always mean you're traveling elsewhere. Being a pilgrim means that you are traversing the landscape in front of you. And there's a big difference between being a pilgrim and being a tourist. A pilgrim soaks in the fullness of the landscape, enjoying and embracing deeply the experience of being present right where you are, whether at home or abroad. A pilgrim not only looks outside oneself to observe what's happening around him, but also looks within oneself to notice what's occurring affectively during that very moment. When I'm in other countries I'm fascinated by virtually everything I'm noticing, paying close attention to what's familiar to me, and what seems brand new. When I'm in different states, cities or towns in our own country, I'm noting what I like and what I'm not drawn to whatsoever. I'm even comparing with what I'm used to at home, considering if, how and why I'd like to live there instead.

Internally, as a pilgrim I'm paying close attention to what brings out life and positive affect as well as what eludes, drowns out or extinguishes my joy. It's all about noticing, paying attention to what births new life from deep within the well of my soul. As a result, what I've discovered about myself is that water in any form is life-giving to me – whether it's the majesty of the powerful ocean, the beauty of a tree-banked lake, the serenity of a trickling brook, the forcefulness of a raging river, the stunning beauty of a waterfall, or even the drops of moisture on a branch or leaf. Water is so essential to life and it appears almost everywhere to provide life to its surroundings. That's why I'm also drawn to the biblical images of rivers, streams, and quiet waters…they all restore the soul and provide life to all with whom they encounter.

Another way my pilgrimage is different from a tourist is during the various and distinct seasons of the year. I love springtime and autumn the best, mostly because they are the transitional times where moderation of temperature and transition of leaves either popping or dropping give signs of life renewed or released. Summer and winter provide the extremes that tend to slap me harder physically and even emotionally. As a tourist I'd just be taking snapshots, treating each as simply a photo op, but as a pilgrim I'm taking seriously each season and discovering the bounty that exists within each. As a New Englander, I have the opportunity to notice the distinctions of each season more than those from other climates. But, also as a New Englander, I – and you – have the privilege of noting the seasons as benchmarks for the region as well as the soul. When does your soul most come alive? Let beauty and bounty grow from within.

30

Creation is majestic and given to be enjoyed

We are created to walk this earth as pilgrims. It's been that way since God first blessed the cosmos with planet earth, creating life in all forms. And, using day to disperse night, water to separate land, light to pierce darkness, plants to flourish the land, fish to populate the sea, animals to co-habitate with humans, and male to be distinct from female, God did it all. The creation story in Genesis is a delightful recounting of how much God loved the earth by establishing it all for our good pleasure, to relish and steward it with gladness and singleness of heart. Creation, including our own lives, is to be enriched by our presence and enjoyed for his glory.

Therefore, as pilgrims who live as active participants in creation, it's incumbent upon us to take care of creation and enjoy it to the max. There is so much to explore and understand about the intersections and interactions within and among God's creation that give us pause to consider. As a family, we've tried our hardest to take good care of our physical bodies, and the land that we occupy. We've sought to be good stewards of the planet, even prioritizing things like recycling and not overdoing the use of chemicals that are harsh on our land. Keeping our yard beautiful, watering and weeding and tending to what's necessary at home as well as helping others do likewise, has simply been a part of our lives. We have sought to teach you to value God's creation, care for it, as God would have you do so, and enjoy it to its fullest extent. There's something extra special about God's creation and we tend to take it all for granted far too often.

So what will be your posture moving forward as it relates to the stewardship of creation? My hope is that you will take care of the climate, honor the life of all, and invest time, talent and treasure to be sure your part of creation is honored as God would call you to do so. And by all means, enjoy God's creation. Hike the hills and pathways into deep forests and high mountains and gorgeous vistas. Sit and ponder the waves as they lap the shoreline. Stare for hours up to the sky and notice the intricacies of the amazing galaxy above. Notice the leaves as they emerge in springtime, come to full strength in summer, turn color and fall to the ground in autumn, and grow under the surface once more in winter. Reflect on the birds and bugs and beasts and beauties that populate our world and are so different from humans. And, take the time and effort needed to care daily for your own physicality and the needs of those closest to you. All of creation is a wonder to behold, majestic and holy, a gift from the Father...for you.

What I'd like to add related to *Pilgrimages Traveled:*

Places I have been, both close to home and far away, that have shaped my worldview:

_____

_____

_____

_____

_____

_____

_____

_____

Travels that have opened my eyes to the gift of creation and the needs of humanity:

_____

_____

_____

_____

_____

_____

_____

_____

Personal values that were most affected by seeing other geography and people groups:

_____

_____

_____

_____

_____

_____

_____

One piece of advice as you are exposed to a wider world of cultures:

_____

_____

_____

_____

_____

_____

_____

Additional thoughts:

_____

_____

_____

_____

_____

_____

_____

_____

_____

_____

_____

_____

_____

_____

_____

_____

_____

_____

_____

Section VII
Biblical Heroes

"Walk with the wise and become wise, for a companion of fools suffers harm."

— Proverbs 13:20

Something to ponder as you read this section: Which of your own biblical heroes would you like to encourage their emulation among the next generation in your family?

31

Ruth the treasured namesake

R uth and her mother in-law Naomi are my two favorite women in the Bible. They rank up there with other female notables like Noah's patient wife, Queen Esther, Mary the mother of Jesus, John the Baptist's mother Elizabeth, sisters Mary and Martha, Mary Magdalene, and Priscilla the missionary, who would also be high on my list. But, as you can imagine, with my mother Ruth Naomi and my wife Ruth Lynn, and my daughter Rebekah Ruth, the choice is clear. The story of Ruth is remarkable from start to finish and has become one of my favorites in all of the Bible. Left as a widow, Naomi wishes for Ruth to go on her own and start a new life. But, Ruth refuses to leave Naomi stating eloquently, "I will go where you go. I will live where you live. Your people will be my people. And your God will be my God." Her faithfulness pays off in more ways than one, and the rest of the story is what leaps in my soul.

Following Naomi and abiding by her well wishes leads her into the care of Boaz, her kinsman redeemer. From the time he allows her to glean in his fields, to the receiving of Ruth as his wife, Ruth takes prayerful risks, which lead her into the protective custody of a man who would invite her out of a grief-stricken heart and into genuine gladness. We know that their shared offspring would lead to the family of King David and ultimately into the lineage of Jesus. Ruth's life was saved, protected, and blessed in astonishing ways, all in fulfillment of God's greater purpose for her life. We treasure this historical record of faithful living and glean from it ourselves as we too seek to honor

God with courageous love and determined fortitude. That's why I call Ruth our treasured namesake, for she embodies what the Ruth's in my life have since emulated.

You both are the children of Ruth and the grandchildren of Ruth, which is a privilege and a blessing from God. To have God-fearing parents and grandparents puts you in a heritage of Christian upbringing and responsibility. We all prayed for you to arrive into our family even before you were in your mother's womb. We have prayed for you each season of your life, during both the good and hard times you've encountered to date. In fact, we pray for you daily, with specific consideration for each of your needs, hopes and various life situations. We have done our best to lay the groundwork for all that God has, is and plans to do in and through you, all for his glory. There was no "magical pill" placed in your mouth that assures your faithfulness to what we have taught, lived, and modeled before you…and so all we are left to do is trust that what was begun in you long ago will be brought to holy completion in your lifetime. May it be so, my beloved.

32

David the shepherd leader

One of God's finest examples of genuine spirituality, authentic humanity, and outstanding leadership is David, who has been one of my biblical heroes since childhood. I recall watching the television show, Davey and Goliath, on Saturday mornings. The claymation format was fascinating to observe, and the truths exposed through the stories that were shared captivated me as a young boy. Then, when I put together the true biblical story of David I leapt over the rather weak imagery of clay into the solid substance of a man who was after God's heart since his earliest years. As I look back on my own life, not at all similar to David's, I too had a heart for God early on. I loved going to church, being with others who worshiped God, always interested in the why behind all the what and how of church life. And, remain to this day grateful for my mother and grandfather who specifically paved the way for me into a life of faith, as well as our church home, even with all its flaws and idiosyncrasies. Biblical characters like David brought my faith to life.

You remember learning about David as a child too. Shepherd boy. Giant slayer. Youngest brother. Chosen king. Saul's jealousy. Jonathan's friendship. Worshiper. Psalmist. Dancer. Lust. Adultery. Uriah. Nathan. Reconciliation. Renewal. The themes of David's life are many, all of which point us toward the Lover of his soul, the Lord of his life, the Leader of his journey. His background as a shepherd boy has influenced me the most. I love the fact that he was the youngest of the brothers, faithful to his sheep, and was called out of a very simple lifestyle to become king of Israel. As a worshiper and psalmist, his writing of Psalm 23 expresses his gentle heart and his resilient leadership. His authorship of Psalm 51 shows us how sinfulness can only be restored through honest repentance. His legacy of spiritual formation and spiritual leadership has marked my life indelibly. The image of shepherd leader is my favorite, for even Jesus would pick up on that as one of his most powerful metaphors for how we mature in God.

When the Lord is your Shepherd, you discover the secret of contentment, rarely being in want. When you trust the Good Shepherd, he is the one who makes you lie down in green pastures, leads you beside quiet waters, and restores your soul. When you follow the Loving Shepherd, he will lead you down paths of righteousness and always for his glorious name's sake. When you believe in the True Shepherd, even when walking down valleys amid shadows of death, there is no fear of evil coming to consume you. He is always with you, his hand and rod will comfort and protect you, anointing your head with oil overflowing. When you know the Eternal Shepherd, his goodness and love will uphold you all the days of your life and forevermore. My children, may the Shepherd of your soul be ever nearer and dearer to you today and always.

33

John the beloved disciple

The beloved disciple John is my number one New Testament hero. He's in this top tier for me because of his desire to come close, draw near, and follow faithfully after Jesus. He's described in the gospels as the one who is closest to Jesus at some of the most intimate occasions between Jesus and his disciples – and not because Jesus chose favorites, but because of John's choice. Specifically, at the Last Supper where he inclined closest to his Savior; at the foot of the cross where he was issued the request to care for Jesus' mother Mary; at the empty tomb when he outruns Peter and his belief is solidified; and at post-resurrection sightings of Jesus when the promises Jesus had declared were all coming true. He was believed to have penned John, the forth gospel, and the final Revelation of Jesus. Each of these encounters and all of his writings, are drenched with holiness and with each recollection I'm profoundly and deeply touched.

The beloved disciple's example to all who observed him at the time as well as for disciples in subsequent generations is nothing short of exemplary. His continual response to all that Jesus invited his disciples to consider was always an enthusiastic yes. I'm struck by his faith in Jesus, and inspired by his example. In fact, my book Becoming a Healthy Disciple is dedicated to his fortitude and decisiveness, for he depicts each of the ten traits of a healthy disciple so well: his life was empowered by the Spirit of Jesus, his posture was one of worship, and his devotion was disciplined and focused; he grew in Christlikeness amidst his band of brothers, and he was loving and caring to all; his servanthood was marked by Jesus' example of foot washing, and his reach was wide for all. In essence, his first century lifestyle of spiritual health and vitality is one I hope many others, including you and me, can follow with all our heart.

To be known as a beloved disciple is the highest form of spiritual adulation even though it's by far the lowest place of humble-heartedness! My prayer has and always will be that you both will pursue this each day. It will be hard in this life, especially given the many reasons to pull away from Jesus and pursue other, but frankly, much lesser philosophies of life. We are living in a polarized culture where people are laser focused on issues that matter most to them, at times to the exclusion of others who simply can't agree: for some it's about their sexuality (sexual preference; sexual identity; male or female dominance, etc.); for others its their political ideology; for still others it's about the cause they fight for; and for many it's all about their work, their portfolio, their possessions, the ladder they are climbing or the social strata they've achieved. To say no to any of these in order to say yes to Jesus first and foremost is difficult to say the least. What will you choose, my beloved children, in hopes of becoming a beloved disciple?

34

Peter the impetuous follower

Peter the disciple of Jesus is one of my biblical heroes because of his passionate and often impetuous actions and reactions to Jesus. I find myself relating to Peter so often as I see him emerge in the gospels and in the book of Acts. His visceral and often impulsive handle on his faith is something that sets him apart from the other more laid back brothers. He's referenced nearly 200 times in the New Testament and is one of the central figures of the early church. In fact, Jesus refers to him as the "Rock" and that's truly what he became over time. His life as a fisherman was transformed into a life as a fisher of mankind, one who would boldly proclaim the gospel of Jesus to all within earshot of his voice. His life, ministry, gifts, temperament and calling place him in the center of the Gospels as a dearly loved friend of Jesus and an amazing Kingdom builder.

Peter has a lot of firsts going for him. His name was always listed first among the disciples. He was in the core group of three, including James and John. He was the first to be called by name by Jesus. He was the first to confess his sinfulness to Jesus. And he was first to promise never to desert Jesus. He received some of the sharpest rebukes by Jesus, and at least seven miracles were performed for Peter or connected to him. Peter is really the most prominent and central figure in the gospels, sans Jesus. He had a passionate friendship with Jesus, and like most friendships there were mishaps and misspoken words that seemed to form an even deeper bond between them. Jesus made a radical difference in Peter's life, and as a result his allegiance and affection for the Savior was deep in return. Even when Peter denies him, Jesus reinstates him and issues him a blessing and sending unlike the others: feed my sheep.

Jesus restores Peter on the shoreline of the Sea of Galilee with the question, "Do you love me more than these?" It's a great question, with three possible meanings to the word "these." One option: Jesus wants to know if Peter loves him more than the 153 fish he just caught and could sell for a profit. Another option: Does Peter love him more than he loves his fellow disciples? A third: Does Peter love Jesus more than the other disciples love Jesus? Although answering in the affirmative each time, Jesus probes his heart for a genuine attestation of his love. The "these's" Jesus is inquiring about in Peter can be linked directly to our own "these's" that may hinder our own affection for Jesus. Do you love Jesus more than your worldly goods or profits; more than you love others; or more than you love your own self? Be careful not to let any distraction outshine your love for Jesus. As hard as it may be at times, may Jesus always be #1 in your heart.

35

Paul the Church and Gospel advocate

L imiting myself in these reflections to five biblical heroes only, Paul the Apostle must be on this list. His dramatic conversion on the road to Damascus transported this hater of the church into her strongest advocate. Barnabas (#6 on my hero list!) was a trusted early church leader and confirmed Paul's genuine conversion, propelling him into the limelight of the 1st Century church. He became a bold contender of the faith, speaking plainly and forcefully about the gospel of Christ. His fearless attitude about the centrality of the Jesus message suited him well throughout his church planting missionary journeys. He is the author of the bulk of the New Testament writings to the churches he loved, and scholars have been confounded since then of his brilliant articulation of so many central issues: salvation, spiritual gifts, the resurrection, unity amidst diversity, church discipline, marriage and family, role of women in the church.

The author of more than a dozen New Testament books, Paul continually spoke directly into the life of the church. His doctrines and practices called the church, its leaders and members, to live with faith-filled authenticity and holiness. His missional focus was toward all who were without Christ in each of the cities and communities he planted new churches. He knew that in order for the world to know of the life-transforming message of Jesus, it needed to be embodied in their fellowships. Harkening back to Pentecost, Paul the apostle knew that without the manifestation of God's Spirit in and among them, nothing would be gained of any value. His emphasis on spiritual gifts, spiritual consciousness, spiritual unity, and spiritual maturity came out over and over again in virtually every one of his letters (also known as epistles).

In your walk with Jesus, it's important that you spend large blocks of time attending to the books Paul has written. Learning the theological doctrines of his writings will inform your views of the world, your community, the church, your marriage and family pursuits, and specifically your understanding of work and your unique contribution to the world. Mostly, Paul will inform your heart about the way of love, which was one of his biggest concepts. Romans 12, Colossians 3 and 1 Corinthians 13 are some of my favorite go-to passages on love. Without love we are nothing but a clanging cymbal. With love we are being fully formed into the likeness of Jesus. Love is what liberates the troubled soul, love is what reunites our fractured relationships, love is what guides our pursuits of holiness, and love is what this world needs more than anything else. Dear children, let the love of God be your guide, guardian and goal.

What I'd like to add related to *Biblical Heroes*:

Biblical characters that have come to mean the most to me:

_____

_____

_____

_____

_____

_____

_____

_____

_____

_____

What I've learned from my biblical heroes:

_____

_____

_____

_____

_____

_____

_____

_____

Ways in which I have sought to emulate the lives of my biblical heroes:

_____

_____

_____

_____

_____

_____

_____

_____

One piece of advice as you discover your own biblical heroes:

_____

_____

_____

_____

_____

_____

_____

_____

Additional thoughts:

_____

_____

_____

_____

_____

_____

_____

_____

_____

_____

_____

_____

_____

_____

_____

_____

_____

_____

Section VIII:
Scripture Favorites

"Do not forget my teaching, but keep my commands in your heart, for they will prolong your life many years and bring you peace and prosperity."

— Proverbs 3: 1,2

Something to ponder as you read this section: Which of your own Scripture favorites would you like to celebrate with the next generation in your family?

36

Psalms – they teach us how to pray to the Father, the Lover of our Souls

Wwwhat will be the biblical texts you turn to as you experience your own aging process? The Scriptures are one of the few gifts we can count on in this world that are both timeless and trustworthy. The Bible is a living textbook, coming alive with each reading and hearing. It's not a dead book, destined for dry, dusty, intellectual study alone. Instead, the Holy Bible is what provides hope to the hopeless, comfort for the restless, guidance for the wayward, and strength for the weary. It's our rock and fortress amidst shifting sands of the culture around us, and it's the primary tangible gift for the soul of the believer bar none. So when I consider for myself the places in the Scriptures that have meant the most to me over the years, I can't help but start with the Psalms, the transformational prayer book that brings me face to face with my Father God Almighty, my Creator, Redeemer, Sustainer and Transformer, the only true Lover of my soul.

In the front few pages of each of my personal prayer journals (for decades handwritten in hard bound notebooks and now found in electronic format in my Evernote app), I have compiled my own list of favorite psalms. They are transferred into each new journal and are simply listed by psalm number, each with its own significance in my spiritual journey. For example, Psalm 23 is my all-time favorite, as it is to so many. I memorized this psalm as a child and each time I read, pray, teach or preach this psalm my heart comes alive with the profound significance of God the Shepherd of my soul. Psalm 139 was my go-to psalm early in my Christian journey, as I was learning what it means to trust the Omnipresent, Omniscient, and Omnipotent God who continually invites me to trust him fully. Psalm 103 provides in clear words the benefits of my soul in concert with the One who forgives, heals, redeems, and crowns with compassion and love. Psalm 16 ushers me into my path of life. Psalm 62 offers me seven life-changing words, "My soul finds rest in God alone."

Holding fast to the Psalms as your prayer book will not only revolutionize your inner life of reflection, but your outer life of meaningful relationships, work, and activity. Your relationship with God will be deepened as you put your confidence in the loving hands of an understanding and empathetic God. The psalms give the believer permission to shout to the Lord in praise and petition, in sadness and joy. They invite us to express the raw material of our lives, offer our heartaches and disappointments to God. And, they teach us how to worship and honor God, both privately and publically, with our words of praise and thanksgiving. The psalms can be sung, proclaimed from the mountaintops, held gently in our prayer closets, and preached from our pulpits, porches and in our family round tables. Start reading and praying the psalms and you'll see for yourself how incredibly wholesome and enriching they will be for today and all your tomorrows.

37

Gospels – they introduce us to the way, truth and life of Jesus

I n the New Testament, my first go-to books are the four gospels: Matthew, Mark, Luke and John. Each has a distinct flair and focus, but all are written so that our intimacy with Jesus can be enhanced. Taking the time to read each of them slowly and prayerfully is the best method for absorbing the richness of the content. I've even taken seasons of my journey to read them in what's traditionally known as the "red letter" approach, reading only the quoted verses of Jesus' actual words. Doing so side by side with various versions is a powerful devotional process, such as the NIV with the Message (not considered a "translation" but a powerful rewrite by one of my living heroes, Eugene Peterson). Absorbing the words of Jesus allows us to enter into the way, the truth and the life of Jesus. The gospels are given to us so to introduce us to the details of what it means to truly be a disciple of Jesus. That relationship is our primary one and is best enriched by prayerful meditation on the teachings of Jesus, our loving Savior and Lord.

The "synoptic" gospels are Matthew, Mark and Luke; synoptic merely means that they take a common approach and are similar in general content. John is distinct in many ways from the harmony of the three synoptics, and paints a portrait of Jesus as God, One in whom we can trust both who he is and what he can do for us. Matthew brings to life Jesus as King, the One who came to deliver Israel, as promised by the prophets of old, and establish his Kingdom here and for all eternity. Mark is the action-packed portrayal of Jesus as servant to all, willing to suffer and die on behalf of his followers. The invitation is for us as his disciples to do likewise. Luke is written by a doctor and therefore gives us intricate details about the life of Jesus as a real human being, interested in the stories of those who surrounded him as friends and followers. Each of the gospels presents the "Good News" about Jesus, but from the various perspectives of the authors, and yet all point us back to Jesus as the way, the truth and the life.

As a new Christian, Uncle Rich took me through an in-depth study of the gospel of John. It is my favorite of the four gospels, but the other three have specific places within where I turn often: the Beatitudes and Sermon on the Mount in Matthew; the incredible stories surrounding the incarnation of Jesus in the first few chapters of Luke; the rhythms of Jesus' work, witness and walk with God the Father in Mark. Seeing Jesus as both human and divine sets him apart as one and only Savior and Lord. Solidifying my devotion to Jesus always occurs as a result of my time in the gospels. Praying into the parables, especially the Sower, the Prodigal, the Talents, just to name a few, encourages me to listen attentively to the deeper meanings of simple stories and to share the gospel with others in like fashion. And, the real life stories of Jesus' disciples and followers invites me into the text as well, whether as a committed lover or even as a rebellious sinner in need of Jesus' new life of grace, forgiveness, and redemptive love. How I pray you too will love the Gospels and mostly Jesus, the center of them all.

38

Acts – they invite us to receive abundant life in the Spirit

I t's amazing to watch the turn of events from the Gospels to the book of Acts. What I absolutely love about the inflection point herein is the incredibly amazing drama that unfolds as Jesus is swept up to heaven and his promised gift of the Holy Spirit is immediately upon his followers. Pentecost comes upon the people in the form of tongues of fire and Peter explains how the fulfillment of what the prophet Joel had forecasted has now come true in their midst! The sign was obvious, the movement of God's Spirit among them was fresh and new and invigorating and renewing, and the wow of God was before them. Repent! Be baptized! Be forgiven! Receive the Holy Spirit! And three thousand were added to their number on that single day. When I consider the biblical text from stem to stern, this single incident becomes yet another major turning point for the faithful ones. And the gift of the Holy Spirit is still available today – my prayer has always been that you too would receive this gift daily.

The result of the movement of God's Spirit among them was a fellow-ship so divine, so stunning, so wonderful, and all because of God's fresh wind blowing in, through and among them. The people of God were devoted to the apostles' teaching, breaking bread together, praying with awe and wonder. They sold what they had and gave to all who had need out of their common offering. They praised God with glad and sincere hearts, and they enjoyed the favor of God upon them all. Best of all: their numbers continued to increase as the blessing of healing, forgiveness and restoration of heart occurred over and over again. The Church has rarely seen anything like what happened at Pentecost, being of one heart and mind, with the grace of God so powerfully at work in their midst. Why? The turning point of Acts 5 tells it all in the story of Ananias and Sapphira: a husband and wife team of deception and greed. The shift from Pentecost to reality occurred when the people of God turned their hearts away from receiving the gifts of the Holy Spirit to the conspiring of selfish testing of the Holy Spirit.

From that point onward, the book of Acts is filled with highs and lows for God's friends, contingent upon their dependence upon God's Spirit or their independence from God's Spirit. It's that simple and yet it's been the same ever since. I choose to highlight this biblical book with one very specific intent: to remind you, my beloved, of the need we all share in common for the filling and refilling of God's Holy Spirit each and every day we have breath to breathe. What's so amazing is that we have this gift offered to us by God to receive, and it's our choice to accept or reject out of our own free will. Whenever I've accepted the gift, my life is all the richer. When I stiff-arm God and reject him out of sheer choice of disobedience or dogged determination to do life on my own strength, I end up driving either on self-made detours or down dead end streets. Please consider daily if you're going to open up your heart to receive the sacred gifts of God (the presence and power of the Spirit as well as the spiritual gifts he entrusts for you to steward) and be filled up to overflowing with the fruit of God's Spirt (love, joy, peace, patience, kindness, goodness, faithfulness, gentleness and self-control). May it be so!

39

Paul's letters – they inspire a Trinitarian With-God life

The Pauline epistles are Romans, 1 Corinthians, 2 Corinthians, Galatians, Ephesians, Philippians, Colossians, 1 Thessalonians, 2 Thessalonians, 1 Timothy, 2 Timothy, Titus, and Philemon. A baker's dozen books in the Bible that amaze and astound scholars, leaders, pastors, and faithful followers like you and me. I mention them in a packet of books, simply to remind you of all that the Apostle Paul contributed to the early Church and subsequently to the historical veracity of the Holy Bible. But, I also want to remind you of some of the key passages that have shaped my life in Christ and my view of the Church over the years I've been a Christian. Without a doubt, my life has been molded, upended, and reformed significantly as a result of an ever-deepening understanding and appreciation for Paul's letters. I still have much to learn from Paul, and will undoubtedly interact with his writings all the days of my life. And I truly hope the richness of these books will turn your world upside down too. What the Apostle urges and encourages are radical departures from all that our world espouses and our North American culture exalts before us. Please don't be swept in to the culture without questioning her values under the microscope of the biblical text. Rest assured: Paul helps us do so.

It's difficult to know where to encourage you to commence your studies and reflections, as each of the books has special significance and focus. Rom.: the plan of salvation; 1 Cor.: the cleansing of the church; 2 Cor.: vindication of Paul's role as an apostle; Gal.: justification by faith; Eph.: unity in the church; Phil.: Jesus-centered love letter to a special church; Col.: Christ as head of the Church; 1 & 2 Thess.: future hope of the coming of Christ; 1 & 2 Tim.: exhortations to a young pastor; Titus: counsel on maintaining good works; Philemon: letter of intercession. And each book has its special highlights, too numerous to mention here. But, some of my favorites are Rom. 5 on justification by faith; Rom. 8 on future glory; Rom. 12 on living sacrifices and the way of love; 1 Cor. 12/13 on unity of the body of Christ, spiritual gifts, and the excellence of love; 2 Cor. 8,9 on generosity; 2 Cor. 12 on power made perfect in weakness. I also love every word in the AEIO books, memorized early on as a believer as Galatians, Ephesians, Philippians, and Colossians. And, as a pastor the personal exhortations to leaders in the remaining books Paul authored have been meaningful at various seasons of my ministry.

Wherever you land in any of Paul's epistles you will discover deep truths that require both study and reflection. Paul had a brilliant mind, which was initially expressed as an outspoken antagonist of Christ and the Church. However, after his dramatic conversion his intellect was transformed by God, radically redeemed for Christ's glory and the building up of Christ's Church. So, don't enter any of Paul's writings without an awareness of the transformational power of the Word. Welcome the insights, convictions, and beauty of Paul's writings as invitations into the deeper life with God.

40

Genesis and Revelation – the Aleph and Omega of our faith

Aleph is the first letter of the Hebrew alphabet and Omega is the last letter of the Greek alphabet. Genesis is the first book of the Hebrew Old Testament and Revelation is the final book of the Greek New Testament. They are astonishing reads in themselves, and are God's bookends to his Holy Word. Genesis begins in Paradise and Revelation ends in Paradise. Genesis includes creation and Revelation espouses recreation. Genesis includes the first Messianic promise and Revelation introduces the final Messianic promises. Genesis welcomes heaven and earth and Revelation declares a new heaven and a new earth. Genesis introduces Adam and Revelation glorifies the Second Adam, Jesus. Genesis is all about beginning strong. Revelation is all about ending strong. Genesis tells it straight and Revelation tells it slant. I'm not suggesting you read each side by side, but instead to be familiar with the importance of both.

As a Christian educator early on in my ministry career, we'd always include Genesis in our curriculum for children. Revelation was saved for the adults, especially those who were smart enough to know how to teach it and handle the questions that this amazing book evokes. But, neither is considered an "easy read" for many reasons. However, they both are essential for understanding our multi-generational faith movement that begins with the dawn of creation and is consummated at the dusk of eternity. Genesis includes the story of creation – both our universe and our humanity. It tells the story of primeval mankind and the history of the chosen people of God. Genesis opens our biblical worldview through the lens of Abraham, Isaac, Jacob, Esau and Joseph...the patriarchs of our Judeo-Christian heritage. Genesis also includes Enoch, who walked with God, and Noah the ark builder, both of whom endured longsuffering with faithfulness. Revelation is all about Jesus Christ and the moral and spiritual conflict surrounding his coming and his second coming. The Lamb is the central figure, mentioned thirty times. Visions are the dominant feature, with varied interpretations for each, since some are veiled and others more obvious. From the messages to the churches in chapters 2-3, to the last 3 chapters of heavenly chorus, marriage of the Lamb, the binding of Satan, and the paradise of a new heaven and a new earth, the Lord is glorified and worshiped.

Entering into both books with both feet and an expectant heart will lead you into the distinguishing marks of faith we've sought to share with you over the years. But, the richness of the Scriptures found in these two outstanding books will blow your mind away over and over again. It's stunning to consider how much God wants us to know about himself when we read Genesis and Revelation. He is our Creator God, who longs to be our Redeemer God, who loves to be our Restorer God, and who freely shares the story of how he has been the Glorified God since the beginning of time and for all eternity. He desires for us to know him, to glean truths from him, to deepen our trust in him, and to celebrate his work in changing lives one generation to the next. We are a part of the great lineage of faithful women and men who have gone before us, and it's incumbent upon us to carry the torch of our faith all the days of our lives and forever.

What I'd like to add related to *Scripture Favorites*:

Scriptural texts that have most distinctively defined my life with God:

_____

_____

_____

_____

_____

_____

_____

Biblical texts that have been most insightful to study and prayerfully reflect upon:

_____

_____

_____

_____

_____

_____

_____

Ways in which the Scriptures have most come alive (preaching, teaching, study, etc.):

_____

_____

_____

_____

_____

_____

_____

One piece of advice as you study, hear, and meditate upon the Word of God:

_____

_____

_____

_____

_____

_____

_____

Additional thoughts:

_____

_____

_____

_____

_____

_____

_____

_____

_____

_____

_____

_____

_____

_____

_____

_____

_____

_____

_____

Section IX
Messages Believed

"Whoever conceals their sins does not prosper, but the one who confesses and renounces finds mercy."

— Proverbs 28: 13

Something to ponder as you read this section: Which of your own transformative messages would you like to convey to the next generation in your family?

41

Becoming healthy

M uch of what I've come to believe to be true has come from my personal experience and my educational pursuits. What I've learned has come from both the school of hard knocks and the classrooms I've enjoyed, from Robin Hood Elementary School in Stoneham, MA, through Junior and Senior High School in Stoneham, and then to Northwestern College in Orange City, IA, and finally to Gordon-Conwell Theological Seminary in South Hamilton, MA. Each place provided for me the intellectual stimulation I needed at the time, combined with the personal and relational experiences that would shape me during that season of my life. I am profoundly grateful for the privilege of learning and all that it entailed, and your mother and I did everything possible to provide for you the best education here in Lexington in both the public schools as well as Lexington Christian Academy and ultimately to Gordon College. Keep learning!

My first book, *Becoming a Healthy Church*, was the coalescence of my academic pursuits and my ministry involvement, in addition to a deep desire to be a published author. I was in the midst of my Doctor of Ministry degree program and serving as President of Vision New England, when at VNE we decided to embark in an extensive research project of what it means to be a healthy church. I was able to combine what we discovered through this research by writing about our findings. What emerged was a book that has been the longest and best seller of the ten I've written to date. What we learned together as a team was that a healthy church was led by pastors and church leaders who both embodied and espoused the ten traits of vital ministry: God's empowering presence; God exalting worship; Spiritual disciplines; Learning and growing in community; Loving and caring relationships; Servant-leadership development; Outward focus; Wise administration and accountability; Networking with the body of Christ; and Stewardship and generosity.

From this first book, I ended up writing a workbook to accompany it, and then complementary texts on *Becoming a Healthy Disciple* and *Becoming a Healthy Team*, in addition to study guides and a handful of devotionals. All of these books were written for Baker Books and LTI Publications, and I hope they will remain helpful tools for future generations of leaders and disciples. Each book was designed in such a way that the reader would come to realize that s/he is a person engaged in a lifelong pursuit of spiritual vitality and maturity. It takes a lifetime to complete that which God is inviting us to pursue as his beloved disciples who are a part of his beloved Church. The message contained within is that in order to become all that God intends, we must first learn how to be as attentive as possible to the work of God biblically and historically, so that we can enter into his-story being written in our hearts and lives as well. Enjoy the journey as you engage fully in the process yourselves, learning and growing healthily all along the way. A daily pursuit of spiritual health is the Rx I hope you'll take!

42

Broken and whole

I'm convinced that God doesn't want to waste an ounce of our pain, heart-ache, weakness, or suffering. His desire is to redeem it all for his glory – if we let him. Learning how to befriend our brokenness, acknowledge its source, discover our contribution to it, and then receive from God all that he desires to make of our brokenness, is the essence of *Broken and Whole*, my second IVP book. It's a message that took many years for me to fully understand and embrace. But, what I've discovered is one of the most life-altering of all the messages I've come to believe in the deepest recesses of my soul. Living in the 21st Century, here in affluent America, we tend to believe that there's no good place for suf-fering - all of it should be relievable. And, in most cases, the brokenness of our world is the agenda we must keep in front of us as compassionate, God-fearing people. Where there is discord, let us sow kindness. Where there is poverty, let us provide relief. Where there is crime, let us administer justice. Where there is war, let us pursue peace. Where there is violence, let us show compassion. Where this is prejudice, let us show love.

But, when there is brokenness in and around us as individuals, families, and communities, the relief and healing may also include some deep soul work. Yes, relieve all that's relievable and strive boldly to do so. But, when our suffer-ing and heartache is upon us, it's important to seek the mind and heart of God on what he desires to make of it. And, it's critical that we look within us to see what there is to learn from our involvement, prayerfully consider the lessons we are to learn, the redemption we are to experience, and the invitations we are to consider from the voice and hand of Almighty God. He is the One who in the first place could have removed it, but instead allowed us to feel the impact and live the experience, so what is the message we are to receive as a result? That's where the deep soul work begins and continues, as we prayerfully ponder the redemptive work of God in, through and all around us, for our sake and most importantly for God's greater glory.

In *Broken and Whole* I introduce the ancient Japanese art form called "kintsugi" – which means, "more beautiful having been broken." It's when broken pottery is put back together one piece at a time, and held together with gold filament, making it stronger than it's original form. So it is with our broken lives, as God comes alongside us to put the scattered pieces back together in a stronger and uniquely more beautiful way. Our family has seen this over and over again, as each of us has experienced our share of brokenness and heartache. But, when we endure patiently and prayerfully through the seasons of hardship, we've seen first hand how God honors our perseverance and blesses us immensely with the richness of his love, grace, mercy and strength. When we are weak, God indeed is stronger still. So, my children, let the love of God be your guide as you allow the Lord of your lives to reign supreme in both good times and hard times, for only then will you know what it means to be broken and whole.

43

Craft your rule of life

Everyone walking planet earth has a rule of life. It's summarized in how you use the 24 hours each day of the 7 days we're given each week. There are times when you brush your teeth, eat your meals, go to work, pay your bills, shop for groceries, etc. and these rhythms and practices, combined with the people you share life with at home, school, work, church and community, are what comprise the details of your personal rule of life. The real question we need to ask is, "Am I living intentionally in a way that honors God and fulfills his purposes for my life?" That's the entre into discovering and crafting your personal rule of life. And, it's the question I asked myself several years ago and have been asking of others ever since. It's a topic I believe in because I've seen the positive ripple effects in the hearts and lives of many who have taken this seriously themselves and have focused time, energy and prayerfulness toward the crafting of a more meaningful rule of life. My hope for you is that you will discover how best to interview the Spirit of God, listen intently to his loving voice of invitation, and respond lovingly and affirmatively to the ways God would have you design or redesign your lives.

What's essential in this process is the ability to listen well. By listening I mean the combination of prayerfully attending to God's voice, as well as paying close attention to the voices of affirmation others have spoken into your heart, noticing what experiences have shaped and strengthened you, and to your inner voice of contentment and discontentment. What is stirring within you and how is God nudging you to consider new ways of living more proactively and ultimately more faithfully and fruitfully? Your personal rule of life is "a holistic description of the Spirit-empowered rhythms and relationships that create, redeem, sustain, and transform the life you are invited by God to humbly fulfill for Christ's glory"(from *Crafting a Rule of Life*). These rhythms and relationships all grow out of one's understanding of the roles, gifts, passion, vision and mission God has created for you to fulfill. Each of these areas takes time to understand, but when considered prayerfully and in the context of spiritual friends, it's amazing to watch it all come together.

In my work with 20's and 30's at Gordon-Conwell Theological Seminary's Pierce Center, I've seen dozens of young women and men grapple with these concepts. I've listened in to their thought process and their prayers. I've seen what they've written up and observed how they describe their rule of life with great intensity and joy. Our team has captured many of their examples and we've placed them on the ruleoflife.com website for others to appreciate and learn from. Most significantly, I've had the privilege of seeing how the crafting of a rule of life changes the trajectory of a life that previously was headed in directions that others thought they should go – parents, teachers, mentors, and coaches – and then shifting more specifically in God's direction too. I've seen how you have chosen various pathways for your life and I'm very proud of what you've learned and accomplished to date. My prayer is that you will continually incline the eyes and ears of your heart toward God's lovingly awesome purposes for you now and in the future. I'm here to help you as long as I'm given life and breath!

44

Spiritual leadership

I n every situation, whether for good or ill, we see the hand of leadership. Someone is always taking the lead. Even in simple conversations among two or more people, we notice evidence of leadership: someone in the circle is ultimately taking the lead. In every sphere of life – business, politics, education, church, and family – someone is seeking opportunity to lead. Some express leadership from the top down that's bold and demanding. Others express their leadership through the coalescing of teams and the empowerment of each team member. Still more may want to be lone ranger leaders, while others are only effective when others are sharing the lead. Regardless of the style or approach, I want you to notice this happening in your life, watching how others around you are seeking to embody leadership – that word or action which evokes a following. And then learning which kind of leadership is worthy of a following, and, what form of leadership you are called to offer in the various settings in which you find yourself. Notice, follow, embody and become the leader God made you to be.

As a Christian, it's important to know what it means to express leadership in a way that honors God and glorifies Christ. It's called "spiritual leadership" (others prefer calling it godly leadership or Christian leadership), because it's leadership that acknowledges the priority of God-dependency prior to and during the process of leadership. When a leader is known as a spiritual leader, s/he realizes that any practice of leadership is a privilege offered by God and as such is to be fulfilled in ways that reflect God. Not much leadership today in our world looks like God! Thankfully, when we look at the life of Jesus and read about the early church and notice how godly leadership has been evidenced in church history and even today, there is much good to glean. Jesus is my role model for leadership and I've enjoyed looking at his life and leadership in the Gospel accounts. There is so much about Jesus that I wish to emulate, and I share this with you in hopes that it will inspire you too.

Very simply, there are three metaphors Jesus expresses about leadership, both in word and in deed. First is the metaphor of leader as servant. Jesus came not to be served, but to serve and to give his life as a ransom for many. Spiritual leaders knows that it's all about sacrificial service for the sake of the thriving of others: are those being served better off as a result of your servant leadership? Second is the metaphor of leader as steward. Jesus taught his followers in parables and urged them to be watchful and diligent. Spiritual leaders know that the people, resources, and programs entrusted to them need to be well cared for: are those being served provided with all that they need? Third, and my favorite, is the metaphor of leader as shepherd. Jesus was the Good Shepherd, and all who followed closely knew his voice. Spiritual leaders know that in order to shepherd the flock they need to protect them from evil, lead them to green pastures, and go after the wayward with a heart of love and compassion. Lead and follow spiritual leadership, my beloved children, and you'll continually live in the center of God's will.

45
Family first

Our priority #1 relationship is always with God. But, second to the Lord is our #1 earthly priority of family. We've taught and hopefully exemplified this throughout your life. Your role in my life is forever and indelibly marked in my heart and soul. You are Mom's and my children, our offspring, our pride and joy. We've sacrificed over the years to maintain this priority relationship and hopefully have instilled within you a commitment to do likewise. You've seen how the majority of our extended family members have joined us in this endeavor to keep each other first and foremost, while others have unfortunately treated us as if we're last on their list. It hurts deeply when you've been disregarded by those you've loved deeply, especially when you know it's not the will of God for families to be divided in this way. How we pray God will break the bonds of pride and bring back that which was once very meaningful with those who have chosen to live in broken and unrestored relationships.

Having said that, let me go back to the priority of family. My mom and dad modeled this in amazing ways. They both came from very different family backgrounds: Nonna from a tight knit "traditional" family of mother, father and brother (Uncle Clyde). They had aunts, uncles and cousins, all of whom (to my knowledge) were in-tact family systems. Papa, however, came from a broken immigrant family. After coming to the USA from Italy, and after establishing citizenship here, Papa's father left the family behind (the rugged details and reasons why are unknown to us). This dramatically impacted his mother's role as sole provider, and necessitated the children work together to help the family make ends meet. The majority of their extended family were still in the old country, so their family needed to hold hands and stick together while building a new life here in the United States. When Nonna and Papa were married, they made a lasting commitment to raise my sisters and me with as much contact with family as possible. They both knew, even from their particular backgrounds, that family matters and no matter what, family was first priority.

So, despite our own lineage and backgrounds, Mom and I have held to this priority too. We've learned over the years that the older we get the quirkier we become. Therefore, we need to cut each other slack, extend to each other grace, and enjoy each other's presence in our lives simply because we're family. And, our extended clan has a good amount of quirkiness to go around, as you've seen for yourself. In addition, Mom and I have discovered, like Jesus spoke of too, that "family" is not only mother, father, sister, and brother, but brothers and sisters as siblings "in Christ," who are from their own natural family systems, and become "like family" in so many ways. You have grown to love these people in our lives too, the "uncles" and "aunts" that have invested in your life through our fellowship and friendship as believers in Jesus. Our Christian "family" means the world to us, sometimes having even more of a heart connection with us than our natural family. May family always remain first for you too, my beloved children.

What I'd like to add related to *Messages Believed*:

Key messages that my parents, grandparents, teachers, mentors, etc. shared with me:

_____

_____

_____

_____

_____

_____

_____

Life messages that have defined my ethics of work, family morals, and life of service:

_____

_____

_____

_____

_____

_____

_____

Messages I wish to convey to you and your generation:

_____

_____

_____

_____

_____

_____

_____

_____

One piece of advice as you glean from the messages of others:

_____

_____

_____

_____

_____

_____

_____

_____

Additional thoughts:

Section X: Practices Lived

"The fear of the Lord is the beginning of knowledge, but fools despise wisdom and instruction...listen to your father's instruction and do not forsake your mother's teaching."

— Proverbs 1: 7,8

Something to ponder as you read this section: Which of your own priority rhythms of life would you like to reveal to the next generation in your family?

46
Scripture, prayer, reflection

E ver since I first dedicated my life to Jesus, my mentors have urged me to spend time in the Word of God and prayer each day. Called at that time a "daily quiet time" it was a discipleship necessity, and became one of the focal points of conversation whenever we'd meet together either in a small group or one on one. All throughout college I sought to make this a daily practice, but never reached the desired consistency of "daily" – instead, "regularly" fit me more appropriately. Ever since then, I have with similar regularity been devoted to this practice. You've seen me slip away from the family routines in order to honor this priority, and you've heard me speak of this and encourage you to do likewise. In fact, I not only believe in the importance of such a "regular" practice, I've even contributed to the genre of available devotional literature written for this purpose – to help others draw near to God in their personal prayer closet. It's there where these "means of grace" (devotional practices) remind us of who God is, what his priorities look like, and who we are meant to be in light of his word.

Spending time in silence and solitude brings us face to face with the stark difference between God and me, and hopefully, in this "crucible of transformation" we are invited in to a new and renewing way of being a child of God. Setting apart a time and place to be alone with God is not meant to instill guilt or remorse about that vivid distinction, but instead to be a warm, loving, grace-filled space where we come to him just as we are. And in that place of intimate fellowship, we are loved on by God through his Word, in prayer, and in honest reflection about who we are and who we long to become in him. To "abide" in his presence, as Jesus invites us in John 15, is to remain in his love not only in that set apart place but each moment of every new day. And as we abide in

Jesus we discover afresh each time that we are deeply loved by God and even though we know our day to day lives don't always show it, we can continually come back "home" to that sacred space of being alone and quiet before and with him. He knows us, understands us best, and welcomes us back into fellowship once more.

The three essentials for a meaningful quiet time are Scripture, prayer and reflection. This has been true for millions of believers worldwide and for generations. Each stream of renewal in the life of the church and all of the saints who have gone before us, and even those who today surround us, would attest to this small list of "must do's." We need the Word of God to guide us daily. The truth of God's Word resonates and comes alive each time it's read and received. As I've grown up in Christ I've practiced lectio divina as my primary way of praying and receiving the Word. In prayer, I've sought to listen to God's voice more than do all the talking to God. If he has more important things to say to me than I to he, then it's incumbent upon me to listen! And, in reflection, a journal works well for me to log my prayers, reflections, confessions, longings, and celebrations. May these simple spiritual practices feed your soul too.

47

Sabbath rest

We certainly were not strict Sabbath adherents all of your growing up years, but you've noticed how important a Sabbath has become to your mom and me. We've sought to set a part Sunday as a special day of the week, meant to break the rigorous routines of the daily in order to focus our attention on God, the people of God, and one another as a family. We've pursued a Sabbath lifestyle for our family for many reasons – most of which are focused around what we've learned from God himself. As we've accumulated knowledge about God's priority for Sabbath rest, we've discovered that it's the turnkey to the deeper life. God practiced Sabbath immediately in the Creation of our world, working for six days and resting on the seventh. He urged his people to honor the Sabbath day and keep it holy, numbering it among the Ten Commandments. In fact, devoting more words to describe its importance than all the other nine. Throughout the pages of the Older Testament God's people adhere to a practice of Sabbath, and when Jesus came he was recognized as the Lord of the Sabbath. Sabbath has always been an important priority for God's faithful ones, and many in our generation are seeking to honor that too. It's definitely not easy in our 24/7 culture.

My friend Mark Buchanan has written my favorite book on Sabbath, called *The Rest of God*. The title is a double entendre – as we learn to rest in God will we discover the rest of God. And that's so true! Sabbath rest is a must for those who want to plummet the depths of wisdom found only in the heart of God. The rhythms of Sabbath, as articulated by Marva Dawn, are four: cease, rest, celebrate and embrace. We must cease or stop what we normally do, in order to enter a restful place, where we can celebrate who we are in Christ (and worship with others who believe likewise), and then embrace once more the fullness of our life with God. Practicing these rhythms weekly, as we do from sun down Saturday to sun down Sunday, invites us into deep rest and ultimately a deeper trust in God. When we put our wholehearted trust in God, we discover anew that we are not God ourselves, nor should we believe we are (even though we act like we are so often). When we embrace Sabbath as a lifestyle we are seeking these rhythms as a day of the week as well as pressing the Sabbath-pause button throughout the week.

Regardless of whether you lean fully in the direction of Sabbath, or simply seek to honor it as a day without work, my prayer is that you will taste and see that Sabbath is good for your soul. And, it's also really good for your relationship with one another as family and friends. Sabbath living brings you in touch with your deepest longings for an authentic relationship with God, as you attend to his invitation into an abundant life. When we pause from our daily labors and notice what's happening within and all around us, we truly discover more of God's creative, redemptive, restorative and renewing work. If we don't stop long enough to notice, we will miss so much about God and our spiritual lives will be more like an inch deep and a mile wide. And so I plead with you, my offspring, to carry on this priority and to do so with rhythmic regularity so that you too will know God at a deeper level and enjoy him all the more.

48

Tithing, stewardship and generosity

G iving back to God that which is rightfully his in the first place has been our attitude about financial stewardship and generosity. We never made a big splashy deal about this with you, but Mom and I have chosen since the day we were married to at minimum tithe our financial resources. In leaner years our net, but most years our gross income, has been given away to our local church and causes we believe in. We've kept track of this monthly and recorded it annually on our tax returns. Making this choice the first week of marriage has definitely made all the difference in the world, especially when the pressures of bills have tempted us to thwart this priority. In this life, despite what the world espouses, what matters most is what you've given away, not what you've accumulated. Jesus was all about sacrificial generosity, and if we're truly Jesus followers, then we need to embrace this for ourselves. What do you wish to be known as: a stingy miser like Scrooge or a generous lover like Jesus? Most of us are somewhere in between the two, stewarding as best we can!

What I've discovered over the years is that there is a big difference between the words stewardship and generosity. Stewardship is more about management of the resources entrusted to our care. Being a good steward is overseeing the limited, finite number of dollars under your control and determining where to place those funds within one's budgeted categories and then overseeing their distribution to your priorities. And, it's very important to know how to be a good manager! But, when we look more carefully at Jesus' economic model, it's much more about how to be as generous as possible with what you've received from your labors. And in this world those numbers will be diversely and disproportionately distributed – from the richest to the poorest among us. What Jesus honors is the sacrifice of the widow's mite, not because she was pitied and had so little but because she gave all that she had away. For the rich young ruler it was nigh to impossible to enter the Kingdom through the eye of a needle, not because he had so much but because he didn't want to give it all away.

If stewardship is management then generosity is only generosity if it has a pinch attached to it. Yes, it needs to hurt a bit to feel what generosity truly is, and that's not often the choice of our heart. But, if we truly want to belong to Jesus and live by his Kingdom priorities, then generosity is the way. So, start with tithing, then review your budget in light of good stewardship, and then pray into where God is inviting you to be more generous, beginning with your financial resources, but overall in terms that describe your lifestyle. I'll never forget meeting Frank, a business executive, who shared with me his desire to annually lower the % of his income he and his family could live on, in order to increase the % of his income he could give away, and before he passed away it was 10% for the family and 90% for others! What a lofty, God-honoring goal, and even though I'm not even close to how Frank lived, that goal remains ever before me. May you be known more as a generous person than any other descriptive adjective!

49

With-God life

S ome believers feel strongly that they are called to serve Jesus and live FOR him each day, being productive and doing as much good as possible for the Kingdom as their daily priority. Others believe firmly that their knowledge OF God is all about using their mind to articulate truth about God and argue in defense of Christian principles. Still others see effectiveness in the created universe as the fruit of one's walk empowered BY God, caring for the environment and all of God's creation. And others will affirm that culture is best transformed through active involvement in political systems, catalyzing change IN God's world. There is another way to look at our Christian life and that is WITH God, being his companion and partner in this world, living out our faith in such a way that others are invited to live WITH God themselves. I prefer the latter approach, which feels to me much more all-inclusive of the above, and alive relationally WITH God (Richard Foster and Skye Jethani have written about the With-God life), as he walks alongside us in this journey called life. My favorite biblical story that teaches this with God life is in Luke 24, as the two disciples are on the road to Emmaus.

The Emmaus experience is rich in detail about the with God life, because first and foremost, it's a reminder that Jesus is always by our side, traveling with us to every destination at every minute of every day. He is an initiator, constantly present to guide, uphold and direct us in our daily pilgrimage. He never leaves us or forsakes us, but instead, he is ever present to empower, enliven, and enlighten us. He doesn't disappear to other continents or zip codes even when we are sleeping. Instead, he is constantly by our side to welcome us into a with God lifestyle always and forever. It's incumbent upon us to remain attentively aware of his empowering presence, remaining alert to his tap, tap, tap on the shoulder of our hearts 24/7. That's truly one of the most amazing truths about God – he's always there, he never leaves – we're the ones who stray, ignore, or push away from him. His ongoing invitation is for our abiding in and staying with him and allow him to take the lead every single step of the way.

"Were not our hearts burning with us?" the disciples asked each other. They were recounting together the moments they came alive to his with-ness in their midst. And that same noticing applies to us today, not heart burn as we seek to lead our own lives on our own strength, but a burning heart in his presence and with his power to calm, comfort, exhort, and sustain. My prayer is that you will know by experience what the with God life looks and feels like, and that you will long for that with-ness in every situation and relationship of life. To walk with God is not only a joy and a gift, but an opportunity and a privilege, not to be taken for granted but to be taken as granted to us generously from the loving hands of our awesome and amazing God who longs for us to be with him every moment of every day. Why? Because he loves each and every one of us more than words could ever fully express or experiences of this life will ever fully embody. Embrace the with God life, invite others to share the journey (family, friends, and spiritual guides like a spiritual director) and you'll never walk alone.

50
Christian community

We are called to live in community, not in isolation. Even God is a mini-community of Father, Son and Holy Spirit. He created us to live in unity, locking arms and walking in sync with one another all throughout life. But, we know that's not always true, as many who claim the name of Christ live very lonely, isolated, alienated existences. This is not always their choice, but instead it becomes their lived reality. However, my experience is that our Christian friends have become for us our lifeline when the going gets rough and we need a listening ear or a helpful hand. As I've mentioned previously, godly friendships are the substance of life, much more than our work, our possessions, or even our achievements. True Christian community is lived out side by side in worship, in witness, even in silence, and of course in service to others here and abroad. There simply isn't anything like the community of the faithful, who know the joy of life together in Christ, and who are willing to take the good with the bad and never forsake the goal of remaining one in Jesus' name.

Even though relationships can be very challenging, it's far better to do life in community than on our own. And, if we want a friend, we need to be a friend – a dependable truism indeed. Doing unto others what we want done to us is the golden rule, which is a two-way street of relational joy. When we have people in our lives with whom we can play and laugh and sing and cry and pray together, then we know we're in a good place in this world. When we feel all alone, it's depressing to know how to respond when all we see around us are people enjoying life in community. Whenever you find yourself feeling all alone, please know that you have friends and family upon whom you can lean. We've had that the entirety of our years of marriage and family life. Without the community who surround us, we would have remained disheartened in times of quiet desperation and in seasons of unimaginable doubt. It's been our friends in spiritual community who have listened intently to our stories, have come alongside us prayerfully, and have served us tangibly with meals, time together, serving our needs, and even finances.

My dear brother Rick Anderson has often reminded me that the Christian community is God's arms and voice for one another. And that is so true, as often we've needed just a hug or a word of assurance to keep us afloat. The Scriptures are filled with admonitions for how best to build healthy community, found in all the one another's of the New Testament (of which there are more than 50 references). We are called to bear one another's burdens, pray for one another, care for one another, forgive one another, and love one another (just to name a few). As a family, we have tried to embody a microcosm of the larger faith community, being there for each other during times of trial and tribulation, as well as accomplishment and celebration. My prayer is that you will always be engaged in community, and that you extinguish the false self of image consciousness and protection, as you light up the world with a true self of communal desire for deeper and more meaningful relationships. May it always be so in your lifetimes and may you multiply this with your children and your children's children.

What I'd like to add related to *Practices Lived:*

Daily and regular practices that have defined and directed my life to date:

_____

_____

_____

_____

_____

_____

What life is like without regular rhythms that help reorder our affections:

_____

_____

_____

_____

_____

_____

Most valuable practices I wish for you to consider in your own life:

_____

_____

_____

_____

_____

_____

_____

One piece of advice as your practices are clarified and fulfilled:

_____

_____

_____

_____

_____

_____

_____

Additional thoughts:

_____

_____

_____

_____

_____

_____

_____

_____

_____

_____

_____

_____

_____

_____

_____

_____

_____

_____

Section XI:
Truths Upheld

"There are six things the Lord hates, seven that are detestable to him: haughty eyes, a lying tongue, hands that shed innocent blood, a heart that devises wicked schemes, feet that are quick to rush into evil, a false witness who pours out lies and a person who stirs up conflict in the community."

— Proverbs 6: 16-19

Something to ponder as you read this section: Which of your own upheld truths would you like to instruct to the next generation in your family?

51

Listen first before you speak

What I am about to share with you here I must admit at the outset: it's easier for me to practice this among those I work with, serve and befriend than it's been for me to offer as generously to my wife and children. Ouch, that hurts to confess, but since it's a truth I believe in, I must address it honestly with you. Regardless of how well or poorly I've done this with you, my desire is always to live out before you the following truth: listen first before you speak. In fact, listen first before you cast judgment or draw conclusion. Listen first because we rarely want to be fixed, but we always desire a listening ear. If you can be a listening ear to another, you are gifting them with something their heart and soul long for: a friend who will listen. There is always much to be shared about life, since there are experiences and relationships daily that need to be processed, assessed, and responded to. Sometimes we get it right at the outset, but most of the time we need space to give voice and interact with what's in front of us (and going on inside and all around us) in this complex world in which we live. When we've been listened to, and sometimes just listened to without any response, we attend deeper to the real meaning behind our words. Clarity comes primarily through the process of listening.

But, listening is not our first or natural response. Our propensity is more toward non-listening. In fact, there are times when we see a mouth moving, but we're preoccupied and elsewhere in our thoughts and emotions, and not really present for the other person. Other times we hear words coming from another, but we're spending our attention energy determining what to say in response. Still other times we're in the presence of another, and hearing their words, but interpreting them even before the full sentiment is expressed, and coming to conclusion about our opinion, recommendation, or response out of our own experience, convictions, or biases. None of this is pure listening and yet we tolerate this kind of interaction with each other all the time and in most of the situations and circumstances of our lives. Let me urge you here to practice good listening skills and know without a shadow of a doubt that the better you are as a listener the richer will be your relationship with God and others with whom you live, work and interact with each day of your life. Listening always trumps a quick or limited response, especially toward those who you know best and love most.

In all the groups we lead at LTI, and in all the one-on-one sessions we provide in spiritual direction, coaching and mentoring, it's always about the listening that makes our times together most meaningful. One friend noted recently that he could find good teaching, excellent resources, and stimulating events in any number of settings, but no one listens to him like the LTI team. Pure listening is a skill to master, an art form of relational substance to acquire, and a personal attribute to develop, since it will affect every area of your life. If you learn now to listen first before you speak, you will be more astute, sensitive, compassionate, and articulate. You will become a trusted person to confide in and follow. Listen well, and pass along listening skills to others you serve.

52

All of life is about trust

Rueben Job is one of my spiritual heroes. He's the compiler of the Guides to Prayer that I've used in my prayer closet and with my ministry teams since I was in seminary in the mid-1980's. I got to know him in the latter years of his life and he became a mentor to me in leading, writing and in specific areas of my spiritual development such as discernment, prayer, and grace. One of his final quotable sayings made an indelible impression on my life. Very simply spoken by this humble man of God: "All of life is about trust." He said this in the context of his illness and his length of years, mentioning rather off-handedly that when he puts his head on the pillow at night he doesn't know if he'll awake the following morning (he only had 25% or his heart working healthily at the time). He was trusting God for every breath he was allowed to breathe. But, then he mentioned that all of life is about trust, not just for our physical wellbeing. Trust is the basis of the complexity of our lives and relationships. When we are in a trusting space, life is good. When trust is bruised, breached or broken, the only way to rebuild it is by trusting God and restoring the trust in our relationships one step at a time. The truth he conveyed has been good fodder for my soul and I offer it to you for the same reason.

Trust is something that's earned over time, and yet so easily dismantled or destroyed. It's strong and tough in good seasons, and finicky and fickle in rocky and unstable times. And yet it is so central and vital to every healthy relationship, and especially with those we know the best and love with the greatest sincerity. The only relationship that's fully trustworthy is the one we have with God – he is truth, trust and trustworthy all in One. All other relationships, even with our closest family and friends, are susceptible to the destruction and disillusionment that occurs when trust is lacking or lost. However, when we put our wholehearted trust in God, we know with certainty that in trusting him with matters of relationship, if all parties involved are willing to engage in the intensity of restoring trust, indeed the trust we all desire can be renewed. That's where hope combines with love and forgiveness and under the prayerful eye of the Father, trust can and does get rebuilt. There's no greater testimony than trust renewed.

In my life I've had both the experience of trust building and trust destroyed. The latter is descriptive of the most painful parts of my life story. Most of the relationships that fell apart have thankfully come back to life and vitality. Those few relationships that were lop-sidedly opposed to reconciliation are indeed the most hurtful. As a public figure in a variety of ministry contexts, I've had a handful of these disappointments. And, our family has endured some as well. But, in each and every situation I can say with honest reflection that I've done everything possible to rebuild broken trust. Some times I've been successful in my efforts; other times not so much. Each time it's occurred has been difficult to fully diagnose; each time they came out of nowhere and were a complete surprise. But, knowing that the abundant life is indeed all about trust, I will do everything possible to speak truth, live trustingly, and pursue trustworthiness all the days of my life, and I urge and encourage you to do likewise. Our #1 relational value is trust.

53

You are dearly loved and deeply sinful

In the world of spiritual formation, we often talk about our true identity in Christ as "true self" and our perceived or desired identity as "false self." Our false self is how we want to be seen by others and so we strive to look, sound, or act accordingly, coming from our self-absorbed efforts. Our true self, however, is best understood in light of a two-sided reality: we are dearly loved saints and we are deeply sinful humans. Growing in our capacity to understand that more fully is how we develop a healthy sense of identity in Christ. We can hold fast to the fact that we are indeed dearly loved by God; he created us, he knows us fully, he loves us completely, unlike any other in our lives. And, we must declare too that we are deeply sinful human beings; we break God's commandments, we pursue selfish gain continuously, we care more about perceived image than humble identity, and we make decisions regularly that displease God and disappoint others. But, knowing we are loved, we are invited to confess our sinfulness and be forgiven of our selfishness, and daily lean into a redemptive state of renewal. That's the sanctifying work God delights to do in our hearts and lives.

In addition to growing in understanding ourselves rightly before God, it's best that we look at others accordingly. Every person walking this planet with us deserves the grace and mercy that God has declared over our lives. Therefore, as we've tried to teach you over the years, practicing kindness and respect to all others is a trait of a man or woman who has deep and healthy roots. Without the need to judge, condemn or force our way on others, it's far better to simply receive them as they are and then bless them with the love of God in

Jesus Christ. That's showing another the hospitality of God, as representatives of the loving Father, the forgiving Son, and the empowering Spirit. Showing kindness and respect to all, means that we treat women equal to men, black equal to white, old equal to young, poor equal to rich, non-Christian equal to believer. The work of judgment, condemnation, and refutation belongs to God and God alone. Our role is simply to live our lives as Christ followers, continue to speak and live out the truth of the Gospel, remain steadfast, earnest and faithful to what we believe to be best about how to live fully for God, and leave all the results in God's powerful hands.

This way of being is so counter to this broken, striving, competitive, divided culture we find ourselves within today. We are urged to take sides constantly, and the loud voice or strong arm of the bully has violated our hope in a more humane society. We are in a crisis of civility today and I want to urge you not to be swept up by it. Instead, I pray you can be more circumspect and even critical of this harshness, so that you aren't drawn in and become as brittle and strident as those around you. You are smarter and more gracious and I'm confident you'll make good decisions for yourself and those you love. Christ calls you to humility, grace, kindness, mercy, and love. For his name sake, Father, Son, and Holy Spirit, and for the Kingdom we espouse for his glory, I pray patience and peace over your heart as you learn how to navigate embracing a genuinely holistic Christian life within this disrespectful and disunited context. Lord, have mercy.

54

God is always good; you should be too

One of the more dominant traits of God is "faithfulness" – he has never wavered from who he is and what he says and how he acts and when he listens and why he loves, and his attributes are faithfully rendered as wisdom, sovereignty, holiness, etc. Yes, faithful he is and faithful he remains, and we can put our wholehearted trust in his hands as a result. The Scriptures are replete with examples of his love and faithfulness, so when you are lacking in faith yourself, you can always open the Word and discover afresh the truth about our faithful God. As the hymn text reminds us: great is his faithfulness, he never changes, his compassions never fail, morning by morning new mercies we see, all that we need his hand shall provide, mercy, love, pardon, peace, and presence he provides, strength for today and bright hope for tomorrow…wow, indeed, great is God's faithfulness unto me. It's because of his faithfulness, that he's good all the time!

Our most appropriate response to God's faithfulness is our faithfulness to God in return. In like fashion, our response to his goodness is our goodness, seeking daily to uphold all that God stands for and invites us to embrace in this life. If you were younger in age, I would include here much more about sexual purity. Being faithful to God means waiting patiently for sharing our bodies with only one, for that is what's good and best for you. Not giving in to the instinctual prowl of sexual temptation and inappropriately expressed pleasure. You have grown up in a sexually expressive generation, where the exploits of others and the implicit messages of licentiousness abound. Sexuality is expressed everywhere we turn, and instead of fidelity we live in a time when anything goes. How I pray God's grace over your heart and body, for protection from the wiles of the enemy who wants to destroy your mind by using your eyes and stimulating your passions toward unfaithful ways that are so not good for you. If at all possible, choose wholesomeness and good old fashion purity, and pray hard for God's strength to reside deep within you so that a firm "no" can be declared to all such perverse sexual temptation. Protect your heart in this way, and do so for your offspring as well.

In addition to purity, I would add a general admonition to goodness as an overall response to God's faithfulness. Being known as a good person means that you are choosing to live a life of simplicity, kindness and mercy toward others. To the broader society, I urge you to remain good to all, paying your bills on time, abiding by the laws of the land, avoiding all appearances of evil, never lying or stealing, choosing not to cut corners, or doing your work half-heartedly. This means that you may have to suffer the scrutiny of others, who will question your motives and manage your intentions toward their gain. But, when you choose to live faithfully before others, your goodness will shine like a bright beacon of hope for all to see. Your goodness reflects God's goodness; your faithfulness reveals God's faithfulness. Remaining faithful to God is the goal, and when your intentionality is focused on God, then leave all the results in his hands. Like those listed in Hebrews 11, it was "by faith" they lived for God. May it be for you as well: live by faith and choose to be faithful and good, my beloved children.

55

Forgiveness is one confession away

L et me declare my apology once more: I'm sorry you were born into such a stubborn family! We can't blame it on the Italian side or point a finger at the Dutch, it's simply what's been inbred in us far too long. Stubbornness is a very real part of our disposition and the ripple effects are evidenced in the need to be right, in control, and getting our way. You've seen my bull-headed stubbornness more times than I care to admit (Mom will have to speak for herself!). Simply put: stubbornness is not pretty, and it's the prime culprit for lack of forgiveness. On the one hand, it's produced a family who knows how to persevere amidst hardship, and that's good. But, on the other hand, stubbornness can be seen in our responsiveness as headstrong, obstinate, and unwilling to confess sin, and that's not good. When we are showing the underbelly of our perseverance, we tend to clench our fists and hold fast to our way, and that will always repel others. Clenched fistedness (expressed in our closed mindedness, unwillingness to admit we're wrong, needing to be in control, etc.) is simply never the appropriate posture within our hearts or toward others. Instead, I have come to believe that God invites us into a life of open-handed love. Then and only then will forgiveness occur.

Jesus exemplified this lifestyle the best when he allowed his arms to be stretched out wide for our sake on the cross. Not only did he stretch out his arms, he received the metal nails of judgment from those who crucified him on that cross. He willingly gave of his life as a sacrifice for all who were desperate for his message of forgiveness, grace and unconditional love. The drama of the cross is what led Jesus into the miracle of his resurrection, and the hope for our eternity. And all of that came in direct correlation to his sacrificial commitment for the sake of our hope for eternal life with him. So, if we're invited to confess our sins before Almighty God, and receive his loving pardon and grace, we must open up our arms widely and be seen for who we truly are. Confess that before God and be forgiven. And, then do likewise with one another.

True forgiveness is indeed one simple confession away from our reality. It's true about our walk with God and it's certainly true about our lives in community. Beginning with the family, and working outward from there, the freedom that comes as a result of genuine confession is the doorway to eternal life found in forgiveness here and now. Entering that door is very hard for the stubborn, hard-hearted ones. For such persons, being imprisoned by stubbornness is what's known and feels safe, and even though the stench is nearly intolerable, it's easier to remain closed-fisted. Let me urge you, my children, to pray into a full release from your stubbornness, and open up the eyes of your heart to see a new and different way: the way of humble admission and confession, the way of open-handed and outstretched arms of love. To live in this way is to learn the way of Jesus, who humbled himself, died for us, and to the glory of the Father, is and remains Lord of all. Let us live fully, abundantly, triumphantly, open-handedly and open-heartedly forgiven and forgiving others for his glory! Alleluia!

What I'd like to add related to *Truths Upheld*:

"The truth will set you free" and this is how I know that's true:

_____

_____

_____

_____

_____

_____

_____

False truths are rampant in our society today; here is how best to discern truth:

_____

_____

_____

_____

_____

_____

_____

Truths I pray you will hold fast to all the days of your life:

_____

_____

_____

_____

_____

_____

_____

_____

One piece of advice as you wrestle with "what is true and false" in this world:

_____

_____

_____

_____

_____

_____

_____

Additional thoughts:

Section XII:
Memories Treasured

"The beginning of wisdom is this: Get wisdom. Though it cost all you have, get understanding. Cherish her, and she will exalt you; embrace her, and she will honor you. She will give you a garland to grace your head and present you with a glorious crown."

— Proverbs 4: 7-9

Something to ponder as you read this section: Which of your own favorite memories would you like to reveal to the next generation in your family?

56
Special and sacred moments

Were I to count up our blessings and memories, they would outnumber the grains of sand along the seashore of life. All the journal pages, photo albums, and homespun movies and videos, do not come close to capturing all that we've experienced together as a family. The special times and even the everyday ordinary experiences of life become sacred moments when seen in the light of eternity. Set apart one by one the number is incalculable, but held as a whole they create a lovely tapestry all held together by the gift of a lifetime of memories. As I recount a few of them here, may they add to your lifelong kaleidoscope of images depicting the myriad blessings of God.

I recall your births, when miraculously you emerged from your mother's body and entered our family life. Nate, entering life after strenuous hours of labor for Mom, and ultimately coming through the help of forceps carefully held by our doctor. Bekah, emerging much quicker, Mom's second delivery which seemed so much easier and less complicated, but equally astounding. Your baby dedications in our church's sanctuary just days after your arrival, are permanently etched in our hearts as important days for the body of Christ to prayerfully join us in raising you to love and fear the Lord. Your baptisms, when you professed your belief in Jesus and your desire to live fully for him all the days of your life, was symbolic of our faith becoming yours. And, your Rite of Passage ceremonies, when you entered your teenage years surrounded by men and women of influence who spoke into your heart and mind about important issues which would mark your maturing throughout adolescence and into young adulthood. Each of these are sacred moments we treasure close to our hearts.

Some of the more difficult moments for our family surrounded the illnesses, aging and deaths of your grandparents. The departures of both Nonna and Papa Macchia were very difficult for you. Watching them suffer at old age, visiting them while they were hospitalized or bed-ridden, was painfully challenging at your tender ages. Seeing them deteriorate in body and mind, was confusing for you because your prior memories of them were so delightful. You didn't want their lives to come to an end, and you verbalized that with sensitivity, gentleness and love. I remember how you held tightly the flowers in your hand as we said our goodbye's to Nonna at her memorial service. And, I recall how touched you were when the military representative at Papa's funeral service handed our family the American flag "from a grateful nation." Albeit very painful moments, they are held as sacred experiences in your growth toward a maturity of heart and mind that would shape the trajectory of your life. You both are compassionate at the core of your being, and I love that about you. Keep reaching out to those in need as you carry on this legacy of family love.

57

Our wedding day

You weren't alive when your mother and I were united in the holy bond of marriage. But, I wanted to include this day as part of these legacy reflections, for it was on July 20, 1979 when the Stephen and Ruth Macchia household of faith was officially begun. There are many treasured memories from this special day of joy. Our love was a young love, which commenced on a college campus in Iowa, on the evening of February 10, 1978, your mom's 20th birthday. We began our courtship the following weekend at the Winter Carnival dance, and we've been growing ever since. We were engaged for nearly a year, mom in Iowa and me at seminary, both of us living at home to save our shekels for marriage. When the big day finally arrived, we were surrounded by family and friends, and were married at First Reformed Church, Sioux Center, IA. The service was followed by a simple reception in the basement of the church, hosted by the women's circle with ham on buns, fruit salad in a plastic cup, blue-colored punch, and handmade mints served to our guests. "Uncle" Henry, my best man, "stole" Ruth after we ran out to the car under a shower of rice, driving off with her in our rental car, much to my embarrassment. All in fun, the ride around the block made for a memory we'd laugh about for years to come.

After a few days of honeymoon in Minneapolis (the closest big city to Sioux Center and all we could afford at the time), we traveled east to settle in married student housing on the campus of Gordon-Conwell Seminary. Mom landed a job at Gordon College, but within a month got a bad case of pneumonia. With no health insurance, and no paid leave, we were immediately behind in our bills. Our newlywed days were strained by a new job, new marriage, new home, new routines, and new surroundings for both of us. After our first year together, we moved to Lexington where we housesat for a family from our church for a month before moving into Buckman Tavern as resident managers. Both Mom and I worked at Grace Chapel, supervised the historic Tavern, and got back on our feet as we shifted from the seminary community to the town of Lexington, the place we've called home ever since. The church leaders enjoyed saying they had a pastor couple living in a Tavern, and it was convenient enough to the church for us to walk to work and experience vitality as a young couple close to the center of town.

From those humble beginnings, our marriage has grown deeper and stronger, both by the joyful and difficult experiences of real life. We made a lifelong commitment at the altar, which would be tested many times over. But, our dedication to protecting one another and preserving our marital fidelity has intensified over the tests of time. Our love is strong, not because it's come easy, but because we've endured some very perplexing experiences and overcome some intense relational and ministry challenges together. In love we came together, by grace we have endured, and unto death will our commitment remain. As a result, we've also experienced more happy and joyful days than the sum of all the difficult ones that ministry and extended family life have dished out. Our marriage and family life has been the centerpiece of our lives and we're forever grateful to God for the myriad gifts that are ours as a result. Praise God with us!

58

Home sweet home

Surprisingly, all you know of a home is contained in one address in our home-town of Lexington, MA. When we moved here in 1984, we had no idea we'd stay as long as we did. We purchased our home through a private sale, from a family we knew at church who were moving west. One of the real estate agents from church volunteered to help us get papers passed, secure a mortgage, and even helped us move in and get settled. I believe she thought her kindness would all come back to her when the time came for us to sell, but that never occurred. We've been here ever since, and have deep roots as a family in this home that we've totally redone and added onto one phase at a time. We fell in love with this Cape-style home, on nearly an acre of land, just a mile from the center of Lexington, with easy access into Boston to the east and the rest of New England and beyond to the north, south and west. An ideal location for us, we have grown to love and appreciate the history of our town and the people of our region.

Home has always been a safe haven from the not-always-safe world. You always knew that from the moment you stepped foot into the front door, it was totally safe for you to be your authentic selves. We have always been free to share the raw material of our lives with one another, and the environment of home has been for all of us a space to be alone in our thoughts or together in our dialogue. We've had great times of laughter and fun in this holy space called home. And, we've had our share of sad anger and emotion packed frustration. It's amazing how both can co-reside in our home, never mind the reality of their co-residence in our hearts. But, we've come to realize that both highs and lows are welcome here in this home that God provided for us to share together for all your growing up years. And, with the rooms not too large, and in immediate proximity to another, we've lived a close family life. And, that's not only by architecture, but by design. We would not want it any other way but close and safe, protected and private, intimate and loving. That's what home and family is all about.

This home has given us many special memories. Most of them contained in the day-to-day activities of family life – meals, conversations, bedtime routines. Homework at the kitchen table was a regular routine for most of your years here. But, in addition, each of your birthdays had friends coming to help celebrate in the backyard or family room. Family holidays have been held here with extended family and friends gracing our presence with their lives and stories. Christmas morning began at the top of the stairs as we'd videotape the mad dash to the mantle for stockings and the base of the tree to be wowed by all the gifts. It was from the front door that you'd leave to drive on your own, take or receive a date to the prom, or depart for college or a trip with a friend. Home has always been a special place, filled with sweet memories of years gone by, and hopefully many more years of memory making in the years to come. Whenever you walk through the front door now as adults you are welcome here with arms wide open to receive your presence with lots of profound love - come back often, ok?! xoxoxo

59

Walking, leaping, and praising God

I have vivid memories of Rebekah's creative play as a young child. She would come up with amazing ways of entertaining herself and others. One of her favorite activities was to use quilts and blankets, chairs and pillows to construct a house in the middle of the family room. She'd bring her teddy bears and dolls into this space and we'd hear her chatter and play with these make believe friends. When her young companions came over to play, they would stay in that space for hours on end. To tear down these castles at the end of the day or week was heartbreaking for her. So much life and excitement had occurred underneath the quilts and whole communities were designed with fascinating imagination. Another of Bekah's loves was dance and gymnastics, and each day was filled with twirl abouts, jumps, rolls, and taps. She took dance for ten straight years, and her year end recitals were some of our favorite times, watching her dance on stage, never missing a morsel of the choreography, taking the lead among her peers.

Nate's early childhood years were a stark contrast to her sister. Four years older than Bek, he preceded her coming into the world with three full years of struggle under his young belt. Diagnosed with a rare bowing in his right tibia just after his first birthday, we began a 17-year adventure together. In that time frame, Nate endured over 250 visits to Children's Hospital in Boston, which included thousands of x-rays, thirteen surgeries, summers lost for the sake of recoveries from those surgeries, more than a dozen braces fit to his leg, more pairs of crutches than we care to count, and middle school and high school years in either a wheel chair or on crutches. Born with "perseverance" as his middle name, he endured these physical health trials and limitations with more grace than one could fathom. When he walked across the stage at his high school graduation, and I was privileged to be the commencement speaker and hand him his diploma, there wasn't a dry eye in the house. A miracle was before us, and with a tip of his cap and a glance to the audience who had prayed for him many years, he walked off the stage with diploma in hand and a new lease on life.

Both of your stories of physical agility and strength came from two completely different story lines. But, both are miraculous in and of themselves. You were both able to walk, leap and praise God in different ways, and both of you did so with more grace than I could fully grasp, more determination than I could ever imagine, and more joy than any other child I know. Watching Bekah on the dance and gymnastic floor in elementary school, or as a cheerleader in middle and high school, and observing Nate on the sidelines as manager of multiple athletic teams during high school, were blissful moments for Mom and me. Seeing Nate walk on his own, and with his right leg still in tact, is nothing short of miraculous. No challenge, large or small, stopped you from being fully engaged in life, even though the abundance thereof looked very different. My pride and delight over you continues to swell upon every remembrance of your childhood, adolescence, and now your young adulthood. Keep climbing, never be derailed, God is with you to sustain you every step of the way.

60
Photographs and memories

F riends and family alike make fun of me for the ways I like to capture special occasions, experiences, travels, and collections. I have more than 50,000
photos and slides accountable online and in photo albums. I've collected mag-
nets from most of the places we've visited across the country and in other parts
of the world. I have patches of the countries I've traveled to around the globe.
Mom and I have collected Christmas tree ornaments since our honeymoon and
on every anniversary since July, 1979. I've picked up rocks and shells from
memorable hikes and on various shorelines. I have a collection of crosses from
numerous locations, made out of wood, metal, fabric, and ceramics. I also
admit to having mementos like small statues of heroes, animals and chachkas
picked up on trips, retreats, or family vacations. I have a few dozen journals
that are filled with notes, pictures, verses, prayers, and sayings that have meant
a lot to me along my faith journey. And, as you know, Mom and I love turn of
the century (from late 1800's-early 1900's) oak furniture, which fills the rooms
of our home. Yes, you might say, I'm a bit obsessed by the value of preserving
and protecting memories.

Whenever I'm asked "why" I'm so drawn to collecting and containing
one's memories, it's because it's so easy for us to forget. God knew this about
his children and used the word "remember" many times in the Scriptures.
Remember the creation as a gift to steward well by filling and subduing it carefully. Remember the Sabbath day and revere it as holy and blessed. Remember
the 400 years of slavery in Egypt, in the wilderness, and be grateful for land
and cattle and life in all its fullness. Remember with a rainbow the floodwa-
ters and how Noah's family salvaged life and spared us from any such mass
destruction ever again. Remember how God fulfilled his covenant with Abra-

ham, and even in his old age gave him offspring that would outnumber the grains of sand. Remember how God brought you through the parted Sea and build a tower of rocks to remind you of God's protection. Remember that we are dust…that we are loved…that we are redeemed…that we are graced with the gospel…that we are going to share eternity with the Father. Remember, remember, remember, and especially remember at the Lord's Supper, the most intimate of love feasts, that the outstretched arms of love were extended on the cross for you. Come back to that table regularly, to remember and give thanks, over and over and over again. Why? Because we have the propensity to forget. And it's better for our soul to remember and give thanks.

Thus the purpose of this book for you, my dearly loved children, my offspring, my pride and joy, my delight. I've written these 60 reflections on the occasion of my 60th birthday for one very simple reason: I don't want to forget all that God has given to our family over the years we've been together, and I want to help you remember and give thanks for the very same thing. We are richly blessed – beyond belief and outside the bounds of what we could ever have asked for, dreamed about, or deserved. But, God, in his infinite love, grace, and mercy, chose to place us together in this generation as the Macchia family. We're no special than the rest, but we are uniquely special in the eyes of God and in the hearts we have for one another. I will always love you and be proud of you!

What I'd like to add related to *Memories Treasured*:

Memories most significantly emblazoned in my heart and mind:

_____

_____

_____

_____

_____

_____

_____

Some memories have been hard to recall; here are a few to know about:

_____

_____

_____

_____

_____

_____

Our family memories have been stored up for you in the following ways:

_____

_____

_____

_____

_____

_____

_____

One piece of advice as you learn to treasure special occasions and experiences:

_____

_____

_____

_____

_____

_____

_____

Additional thoughts:

About the Author

Stephen A. Macchia is the delighted husband of Ruth and the proud father of Nathan and Rebekah. He grew up in an imperfect yet loving family in a suburb of Boston, Massachusetts. After high school, he ventured to the Midwest where he attended Northwestern College in Orange City, Iowa sight unseen and at the encouragement of his mentor. Upon graduation, he moved back to Massachusetts where he attended Gordon-Conwell Theological Seminary in South Hamilton, MA. where he subsequently earned his Masters of Divinity and Doctor of Ministry degrees. During his seminary days he began a wonderful tenure of service on the pastoral staff of Grace Chapel in Lexington, MA. In their first few years of marriage, Ruth and Steve also were privileged to serve as Resident Managers of a historical home in Lexington before moving to their current home more than three decades ago. From Grace Chapel, Steve was commissioned to lead the 100 year old Evangelistic Association of New England, which became Vision New England under his tutelage. In 2003, Ruth and Steve ventured into the world of ministry entrepreneurship by founding Leadership Transformations, Inc. (LTI).

Steve is the author of several books, including the Baker bestseller, *Becoming A Healthy Church*; IVP titles, *Crafting a Rule of Life* and *Broken and Whole*; as well as an assortment of additional books, workbooks, and devotionals:

Becoming A Healthy Church Workbook
Becoming A Healthy Disciple
Becoming A Healthy Disciple Small Group Study and Worship Guide
Becoming A Healthy Team
Exercises for Becoming A Healthy Team (co-author)
Wellspring: 31 Days to Whole Hearted Living
Path of a Beloved Disciple: 31 Days in the Gospel of John
Outstretched Arms of Grace: A 40-Day Lenten Devotion

Steve Macchia can be reached via the Leadership Transformations ministry website: www.LeadershipTransformations.org

LEADERSHIP
TRANSFORMATIONS INC.

- Soul Care Retreat and Soul Sabbaths

- Emmaus: Spiritual Leadership Communities

- Selah: Certificate Program in Spiritual Direction (Selah-West, Selah-East)

- Spiritual Formation Groups

- Spiritual Health Assessments

- Spiritual Discernment for Teams

- Sabbatical Planning

- Spiritual Formation Resources

Visit www.LeadershipTransformations.org
or call (877) TEAM LTI.